SHARING THE
Feast

For Mary Bunnell and Alfred Robbins

*Who, in different ways,
have shared their feasts with me*

SHARING THE Feast

ANNA ROBBINS

Authentic

SPRING HARVEST
Equipping the Church for action

11 10 09 08 07 06 05   7 6 5 4 3 2 1

First published in 2005 by Spring Harvest Publishing Division
and Authentic Media, 9 Holdom Avenue, Bletchley, Milton Keynes,
Bucks MK1 1QR, UK
and 129 Mobilization Drive, Waynesboro, GA 30830-4575, USA
www.authenticmedia.co.uk

British Library Cataloguing in Publication Data

A catalogue record for this book is available from the British Library

ISBN 1-85078-635-6

Cover design by fourninezero design.
Typeset by Waverley Typesetters, Galashiels
Print Management by Adare Carwin
Printed by Haynes, Sparkford, Yeovil, Somerset, UK

Contents

Acknowledgements

It seems that everything I write bears the fingerprints of my own teachers. I hope they do not mind if I appear to plagiarize their work from time to time. Their thought has become such a part of my own thinking that I find it difficult to distinguish where their ideas end and mine begin. Yet, they are not to be blamed for my failings in understanding or communication. They include those who provided building-blocks for me at Acadia Divinity College in Nova Scotia, Canada, and those who later helped me to put them together, particularly my theological mentor, Alan Sell. His influence marks most pages you will read here, and I hope that does not horrify him too much.

I am grateful to the London School of Theology for providing regular sabbaticals that allow research and writing to be done in a time-out from regular lecturing responsibilities. In particular, I thank Derek Tidball for his support and Conrad Gempf for debate and encouragement. The members and friends of the Beechen Grove Baptist Church provide the context where much of my 'academic' thought hits the ground. I deeply appreciate their openness and faithfulness, allowing me to air my ideas and wrestle with how they work out in real life. I hope they won't mind to find themselves hidden in these pages occasionally.

The manuscript was much improved by David Sanders' careful attention, and Stephanie Heald at Spring Harvest Publishing made the project possible by seeing something of value in the vision, and driving it forward.

My long-suffering husband, Peter, not only tolerated an intense writing period, but he also read the manuscript as it was produced, and made helpful comments. His partnership in the gospel is vital to me, and everything that I do. And I thank God for letting me do things that I love.

Introduction

Who would you invite to your perfect dinner party? Would it be a famous character from the annals of history, like Columbus or Churchill, or maybe a biblical figure like King David or the apostle Paul – haven't you always wanted to ask him what his thorn in the flesh was? Maybe you'd invite your favourite film star, or a political hero. Perhaps you'd just like to gather with your closest friends and family, and laugh together, and feast.

Maybe the idea of hosting a dinner party fills you with dread. After all, we're not all domestic gods or goddesses who adore creating perfect dishes to serve on the perfect table to the perfect selection of dinner guests. What would you cook? Where would you shop? What recipes would you use? How would you present your dishes? What if the guests have allergies, or are fussy eaters? What if something goes wrong and the whole evening is ruined? Maybe you should just forget it. Phone for a takeaway and plop down in front of the TV instead. Whew! What a relief.

The way we relate the gospel to the world today is much like hosting a dinner party, or serving up a feast. For some, it's the school dinner approach: take what's on offer, like it or lump it. Everybody get in line, take your portion, and move along. For others, it's like an all-you-can-eat buffet where hundreds of dishes are laid out alongside one another, and you can pick and choose what you want according to your individual taste. For others still, it's like going home to a Christmas feast, where the traditions are lived out, year after year, but with a new twist here, and an experiment there. It's interesting and creative, but reliable, right down to the Brussels sprouts everybody loves to hate.

Too often, the very thought of the effort required to present the gospel to unfamiliar taste buds is overwhelming, and so we don't bother. If we do decide it's worthwhile, we may engage the task of inviting the people of our culture to the banquet with fear and uncertainty. It can be a risky, ineffective and exhausting venture. Struggling to prepare a feast for our culture can create an imbalance in our own diet, and it can so easily go completely wrong.

When I was a child, my mum spent a lot of time in the kitchen. We didn't have much money, so she baked everything herself. Biscuits, cakes, breads, you name it. I have fond memories of chocolate and walnut dreams, crispy chocolate chip cookies hot out of the oven, a slice of warm bread dripping with butter.

But not every baking adventure was a success. During one particular health food phase, we had carob instead of chocolate, and soya grits with everything. Soya grits with macaroni, soya grits and vegetables, ice cream with soya grits. Yuck. One day I remember venturing into the kitchen, where Mum was proudly removing her first carob cake from the oven, to serve to guests that evening. It looked and smelled like chocolate. So far so good. She decided she wanted to try her new recipe for soya icing, but realized too late that she didn't have any more grits, or any tofu. Never mind, she thought. I must have a substitute. She rifled through the cupboard, and emerged holding aloft a large bottle of Chinese soya sauce. Soya bean curd, soya sauce. Same name, what's the difference? I can assure you the difference stayed with us for ages after eating our one and only slice of cake with soya sauce icing! Some of us still can't look at a piece of chocolate cake without thinking of kung pao chicken.

On another occasion, Mum was kneading the bread she baked every week, when she realized the bandage she'd put on her finger was missing. 'Never mind,' she thought, when she couldn't find it. 'If it's in the bread, the heat of the oven will sterilize it, and I can throw the loaf away when it appears.' She proceeded to let the bread rise, punch it down, and let it rise again. Finally, her morning's work was finished, and six beautiful loaves emerged from the oven. Our neighbours dropped by, and so we cut into the first steaming loaf, and began to eat. Our faces screwed up in disgust. It tasted like rubber bandages! 'Ah, we found it,' she said, and threw the loaf away. We cut into the next loaf, but again, the taste of medicinal rubber permeated the flavour. We continued to slice through the entire batch until she realized that the taste of the bandage had penetrated every loaf. And we thought a little *yeast* could work through the whole dough!

Despite these occasional disasters, Mum didn't give up cooking, much to the relief of those of us who needed to eat! Often, as the church, we're so discouraged by failures of trying to relate the gospel to the culture in which we live, that we do give up. Yet there are hungry hoards still waiting and wondering when the dinner gong will sound. They need to be fed, but some of us are scared. Out of our fear, we close the restaurant, or we agonize about the task so much that we offer only tiny nouvelle-cuisine portions. The starving need to eat, but some of us are serving an imbalanced diet, and they're going away still malnourished, while we are bloated from feeding at the trough.

A college friend used to love to cook, but she would spend all day in the kitchen, dirtying every dish in the house. She'd feast as she went along, tasting this, and trying that. Finally, when all of us were hovering at the table, famished, and wondering when the feast would begin, she would emerge with her masterpiece which was usually a single dish, sufficient for only one or two people. She'd worked all day and her appetite was satisfied, but the rest of us still had to send out for pizza! As the church, we may not find it desirable to produce an all-you-can-eat buffet to suit all taste buds, and we can't force-feed people who simply don't want to eat. But we can take a few recipes that have been handed down through the generations, and make them live again in the present. We can enjoy the experience of cooking, and make sure there's enough to go around. We can make sure we're ready, steady, and cooking the gospel for our culture today.

The implications of this go beyond our approach to evangelism to the way we understand discipleship. The way we understand the gospel in the contemporary era reflects back on the very nature, purpose, and shape of the church itself. It involves every area of our faith, and what we believe about God. Should we find out what the diners find appealing, and transform our entire faith menu in response to their desires? What if they don't like fruit and vegetables – aren't we cheating them, and us, out of a balanced diet by excluding nutritious foods? What if they've never heard of the delights of truffles, and chocolate pudding? Aren't we robbing them of experiencing some of the best culinary delights by not putting them on the table?

Similarly, if the contemporary world understands little of sin, and self-sacrifice, should we simply talk about love and friendship, and leave the cross off the menu? Or if the culture resists commitment should we stop talking about meeting together and talk about takeaway church instead? Which parts of our belief and practice can we adjust in response to cultural shifts, and which recipes would be disasters if they were changed? How much are these questions themselves products of a culture that challenges everything, and to what extent is the faith we have timeless and unaffected by cultural influences? The way we answer these questions will influence the shape of the church and the form of our beliefs.

WHICH PARTS OF OUR BELIEF AND PRACTICE CAN WE ADJUST IN RESPONSE TO CULTURAL SHIFTS, AND WHICH RECIPES WOULD BE DISASTERS IF THEY WERE CHANGED?

I knew a man who was an excellent chef. Every time he cooked for a dinner party or a church supper, everyone would rave about what splendid dishes he'd come up with. Of course, he was inundated with requests for copies of his recipes, and he happily obliged. But after a few years, people started to become suspicious. No matter how closely they followed the recipes he'd given them, the dishes never turned out as well as his. Eventually he admitted that when he gave out a recipe, he made slight changes to the quantities of some ingredients, so that it would never turn out as well as when he made it. Even small changes made a difference to the final outcome.

We once compiled a church cookbook as a fundraiser for a mission project. As time went on, a number of typing errors were pointed out to the editing team. One recipe for a cake was missing any dry ingredients. Another for salad dressing had left out the oil. Like these recipes, when a major ingredient is missing from our faith and culture recipe, it can turn out to be a disaster. Some ingredients are essential, and can't be removed or altered. But sometimes, adding a fresh ingredient can give the recipe spice or zest, and be just the thing needed to make a dreary recipe come to life. A little imagination and creativity can go a long way.

So how do we learn which ingredients are essential, and which ones can be altered? How do we respond to the culture in ways that are both effective for contemporary palates and faithful to the ingredients that are prescribed for our good health as Christians? How do we decide which traditional recipes need adjustments, or ought to be rejected, and which ones are perfect just as they are? Or is it just a matter of laying out the ingredients, and letting everyone mix their own?

This is the art of theological cookery, and I invite you on this course with me. Here, we'll examine the challenge of relating faith and culture, explore which ingredients are given, and which ones change with the world around us. First we'll assemble the staple ingredients – those that form a biblical understanding of the content of the gospel, and inform our communication of it. They include the main biblical teachings about human existence and our relationship with God.

Then we'll gather the seasonal ingredients – those that form the culture in which we live, and inform the way we respond to it. Like all good food courses, we'll look at some of the new ingredients available in culture today, and trace some of their origins. We'll consider what the taste buds of today find palatable, and why. And then we'll mix some of these things together, and see what our contemporary recipes might look like. Hopefully, you'll feel encouraged, and equipped for your own encounters with culture as a confident, and not arrogant, Christian. Maybe you'll even be inspired to host your own experimental dinner party, where you can cook up a storm, and invite those who have never encountered Christ to a feast where they can 'taste and see that the Lord is good'.

Ultimately, the feast is God's and the table is his. We simply serve as sous-chefs. It can be challenging, and fun, and most certainly adventurous. It's time to assemble the ingredients. Get your apron on, grab a cappuccino, and join me in the Kingdom kitchen.

1

Assembling the Ingredients: From the Store Cupboard

1

Assembling the Ingredients:
From the Store Cupboard

John Lennon's song *Imagine* was declared the anthem of the millennium by culture watchers. Hailed as a secular hymn of the age, the song was an indictment of religious belief, and expressed a desire to transcend the conflict and materialism of this world. Wouldn't it be great if we could live in a world where there was no religion, no war, no money, and everybody just loved each other? It's difficult to disagree with such sentiments. But a little reflection leads us to conclude that regardless of how much we like to hum the tune, the song is actually a caricature of the world it paints. It doesn't take a genius to look around the world and figure out that it's a far cry from this dreamy ideal. Take away religion, money, and the hope of heaven, and people will still find means to accrue wealth, ways to exploit others, and reasons to fight. Lennon's widow Yoko Ono must have realized this when she licensed a number of baby products to be produced and marketed under the Imagine brand.

TAKE AWAY RELIGION, MONEY, AND THE HOPE OF HEAVEN, AND PEOPLE WILL STILL FIND MEANS TO ACCRUE WEALTH, WAYS TO EXPLOIT OTHERS, AND REASONS TO FIGHT.

Nevertheless, the popularity of the song testifies to the fact that we all have hopes and dreams for this world. We seek after meaning, purpose, and direction, and we find it in different places. But we all believe *something* about how and why the world exists at all.

Everybody has religious beliefs. Everybody believes something in response to the basic questions of life, 'Who am I? Where am I going? Why are we here?' even if the answer is simply 'I don't know.' The form that the answers to these questions takes is what defines our religious belief. More specifically, what we think about God and the way he relates to the world, is the content of our *theology*.

Our beliefs about God, Jesus, the Holy Spirit, and ourselves make up the staple ingredients with which we will prepare recipes for our feast. In our discipleship, and evangelism, how we understand and use these 'store cupboard' ingredients will determine the overall flavour and texture of the dishes we prepare, and the way we serve them to others. It's appropriate, then, that we start here. We have to take stock of what we believe, so that we're consciously aware of the range of possible traditional ingredients that we will have available to mix with other local and seasonal ingredients later.

As Christians, we base our understanding of God and ourselves on the Bible. We believe the Bible to be a reliable account of God's dealings with humanity. As such, it records how he showed himself to people in the past, and is one of the ways he continues to show himself to people today. Sometimes, we find it hard to relate the Bible to people who aren't Christians. Either we're not familiar enough with what it contains, or we're afraid of sounding like we hail from another century, not at all in touch with today. In either case, we can easily reduce our beliefs to cheesy slogans or trite comments that don't really address the challenges we face.

To allow the Bible to speak to contemporary audiences, we need to know and understand what's in it. More than that, we need to consider the Bible as a whole and not simply cherry-pick verses to throw at people as they walk past, in a blind hope that something will stick. Looking at the Bible as a whole gives shape to the things we believe and helps us move beyond the throwaway catchphrases that don't really mean anything. We can define a structure that gives our faith backbone and form. It may not define everything down to the last muscle and sinew, but it will give us enough to trust in its sufficiency in the face of constant cultural challenges.

Recently I met someone who is not yet a Christian. She told me that she was driving down the high street, when a car came up behind her, shunting erratically all over the road. She pulled up to allow the car to pass. Inside, the driver was chatting on his mobile phone, while leaning back and dealing with three kids in the back seat. As the car sped past, my friend caught a glimpse of a sticker encouraging her to 'Smile! Jesus loves you!' She told me, 'That may well be true, but I don't want to meet him face to face just yet!'

It's not good enough for Christians to simply turn our faith into a battery of slogans that we think serve to answer the deep questions of people in today's world. It's not good enough for them, and it's not good enough for us. No wonder people think that the Christian faith offers simple answers, if that's all we ever give them. What we believe about God, about ourselves and the world, largely determines how we engage our culture. That's why these are the *stock* ingredients; they are comprised of familiar affirmations that give us somewhere to put our feet, even in the midst of shifting sands. They are central to our belief and deserve understanding.

At the same time as we're throwing popular slogans around, myths are springing up that attempt to explain aspects of human existence and history. They are embraced by our culture, and they often go largely unchallenged by Christians. Usually we prefer to ignore them, and if we do address them, we don't allow our biblical understanding to set the agenda. Let's examine a few popular myths together, organized around the narrative of the Christian story. Together we'll see how we can move past them to a deeper understanding of the basic ingredients of Christian belief.

Creation v. the myth of mindless evolution

'Some call it evolution, and others call it God,' so said William Herbert Carruth.

This oft-cited quotation represents a trite summary of our beliefs about creation when confronted by challenges from the realm of science. Evidence for evolutionary theory, and the rugged biological interpretation of every aspect of human behaviour, leaves us feeling little more than glorified apes. With scientists telling us that everything we do is based on our evolutionary biological need to reproduce, sex becomes the central focus of human nature and development. It shouldn't surprise us when we hear the lyrics of a song proclaiming, 'You and me baby, we ain't nothin' but mammals, so let's do what they do on the Discovery channel.'

As Christians, we often don't face this challenge head-on, but simply keep insisting that we're creatures, not mere products of evolution. While we battle over the logistics of how creation unfolded, we may make newspaper headlines, but we're losing out on an opportunity to consider positively what creation *means*. It's hard for us to move past the Sunday school affirmations that 'God made the flowers, God made the trees and God made me.' We whistle their ethereal tune in the dark while surfing the web for the next hit of stimulation. And yet, these same affirmations open a great door into scriptural under-standings of what it means to say that we are *creatures* and not accidents.

> THE FACT THAT WE HAVE THE CAPACITY TO BE INTIMATELY RELATED TO GOD IN OUR EXISTENCE IS BASIC TO WHAT IT MEANS TO BE HUMAN.

The fact that we have the capacity to be intimately related to god in our existence is basic to what it means to be human. The physicist Paul Davies recognizes the uniqueness of human consciousness and its significance as a fact of life. In *Mind of God*, Davies wonders at why it is that '*Homo sapiens* should carry the spark of rationality that provides the key to the universe'. To him, it is 'a deep enigma'. He goes on to ask in his final paragraph

> What does it mean? What is Man that we might be party to such a privilege? I cannot believe that our existence in this universe is a mere quirk of fate, an accident of history, an incidental blip in the great cosmic drama ... The physical species *Homo* may count for nothing, but the existence of mind in some organism on some planet in the universe is surely a fact of fundamental significance. Through conscious beings the universe has generated self-awareness. This can be no trivial detail, no minor byproduct of mindless, purposeless forces. We are truly meant to be here.

Regardless of whether you believe that God created through evolution or through a big bang, the reality that God is the source of all life is not an inconceivable truth, but crucial to a fully-orbed faith. The Bible contains many forms of literature – poetry, prose, prophecy. But it is not, nor does it pretend to be, a science book. Biological principles might be helpful for understanding the mechanics of the world in which we live. Yet the Bible moves us to consider the 'why' behind our existence, and bears witness to the deeper principles of human nature and destiny.

There are a number of things we can confirm as a result of what the Bible teaches about God's creative activity. The fact that God created means that there is goodness in the things he made (Gen. 1:31). Because he made us in his image, we are related uniquely to him (Gen. 1:26–30) and to other people, regardless of whether they are Christians or not. We are also connected intimately to the wider created world, and have special responsibility to look after what God has made. We are able to enjoy God's good creation, to be nurtured by it, and to be stewards of it. We're responsible to God for how we use his gift of earth and all that's part of the natural world. We're not 'just mammals' but intelligent, moral, relational beings.

Through creation, God tells us something about himself, his nature, and how he relates to the things he's made. We know he loves us, because he provides enough for the needs of his creatures. We know he cares for us, because he sustains his creation (Ps. 104:10–30). We know he is personal because he walked with his human creatures in the intimacy of the garden of Eden. We know he's relational because he made them to love him freely. Even at creation, God's threefold nature was present and active. Jesus was the firstborn over all creation, and he was involved in everything that was made, and is the initiator of a new creation (Col. 1:15–17). The Spirit hovered over the waters at the first creative moment, and brings the spark of creativity to us every morning (Gen. 1:2; Ps. 104:30; Lam. 3:23).

Being creatures means that we are related to our Creator. We bear his image, which includes the moral capacity to relate or to rebel, to reason or to run. Our relationship with God is based on moral categories, whereby there are patterns of behaviour that cause the relationship to thrive, and ones that cause it to fracture. Being created, rather than being an accident, means that there is purpose and direction to our living that stands beyond our own striving to discover and create. It also means that there are guidelines, or parameters for healthy living, given by our Creator. When you buy a new toaster, it usually comes with instructions for maintenance and operation in order for it to function at its best. As creations, we are similar. We are well-designed, with potential for full life and goodness. Our goodness is brought out best when we operate under the guidance of the Creator. Being created means we come with instructions.

Remember that classic film, the 1968 version of *The Planet of the Apes*? It was based on the novel *Monkey Planet* by Pierre Boulle. In the movie, Dr Zaius is an ape, a leading scientist, and also guardian of the faith for an entire civilization of apes. On their planet, humans are scorned, and not considered to be reasonable or spiritual beings, but simply savage animals. When a man, Taylor, crashes his spaceship on the planet, he is caged, observed, and eventually tried in court. Taylor claims to be intelligent and reasonable, and accuses the apes of being culturally backward for having their scientific enterprise so closely allied with their religious beliefs. He believes Dr Zaius uses religious belief to block knowledge and prevent progress. Moreover, he sees how Zaius' religion justifies his prejudice against humans. As viewers, we feel drawn into a critical angle on religion along with the hero of the story. The apes should listen to the man, and recognize how deluded they are.

At the end of the film, however, things are turned upside-down. Taylor has been left to wander the 'forbidden zone' of the planet, where he sees a large structure emerging from the sand by the seashore. Slowly the camera pans out, and we recognize the arm and head of the Statue of Liberty. In that moment, Taylor realizes that he has actually landed on his home planet, in the future. Humans had destroyed their civilization through nuclear warfare. The planet is now run by a civilization of evolved apes. In the screenplay by Michael Wilson, Taylor crouches in the sand and shouts 'My God!' In the film, we hear the famous lines shouted angrily, 'Damn them! Damn them all to hell!' In either case, the man is left acknowledging the necessity of a moral sense for human existence.

The separation of morality from action was what made humans nothing more than animals. Conversely, what made the apes more human than the humans was their moral sense, the very thing that the 'rational' humans who destroyed the planet had lost. They had a sense of what was right and wrong, and acknowledged an authority outside of themselves. They were committed to these ideals as preservation against self-destruction. They knew they needed to look to something bigger than themselves in order to maintain the quality of their existence. They needed instructions.

Crash v. the myth of human goodness

As the author of creation, God has authority to determine how it should function. He has designed the world with purpose, so that our lives are more than roulette wheels of chance. Like the author of a story, he has the sovereignty to determine the overall shape of the plot and the way that the characters should behave. Unlike the author of a story, he has given us the freedom to dance to his rhythms of creation, or to wander humming our own tune.

A musician I know was invited to play a minor role in a film following the life of an historical character. The film was being shot on the estate of a well-known man of noble descent. My friend was to play an antique organ in one of the rooms of the historical house, where the main character would enter and admire the instrument. He located some music appropriate to the era, and was kitted out in period costume. Just before shooting began, a phone call came from the lord of the manor, who insisted that under no circumstances was anyone to touch his beloved organ, save for a member of his own family, lest they break it. Needless to say, the director was frustrated, and my friend disappointed.

As God's creatures, we are precious to him. But unlike this lord, our Lord doesn't claim his right to possess his treasures. He allows them to enjoy life freely, and with this comes the risk that some things might get damaged or broken. And sadly, we did break our relationship with him. It was violated when humanity became unfaithful in our relationship with our God. It is violated when we are unfaithful to him in our own lives. As humans, we desire so much to enjoy creation, that we forget our Creator. Marcel Proust suggested the possibility that 'the highest praise of God consists in the denial of Him by the atheist who finds creation so perfect that it can dispense with a creator'. Despite his sentiments that express appreciation for the natural world, relating to God properly requires our acknowledgement of his sovereignty as our maker.

When an artist displays a painting, he runs the risk that it will be wrongly interpreted. It may be hard for him to let go, because it bears his fingerprints. And yet, that's part of the reason he paints – to express himself, and allow his talents and insights to be enjoyed by others. To experience the beauty of the work, you have to come to it freely, without the artist forcing an interpretation upon you. But there can be guidance that assists your interpretation, and leads you into a deeper appreciation of the work.

If you've ever visited the Tate Modern in London, you'll know what I'm talking about. Wander around and look at the art. Some of it is repulsive, some of it inspires. Some pieces are lenses to beauty, and others make you weep with despair. Many are confusing. How many times has it happened that you look at a sculpture, or film or painting, and no matter how long you gaze, you are unable to connect with the work at all? Then, you go to the little panel on the wall and read about the piece, or listen to the audio guide. Suddenly, a new light is offered that helps you make sense of the alien forms in front of you. It may limit your freedom to interpret the work as you choose, but the artist (and the curator) has the authority to decide whether to direct you into the work, or to let you flounder on your own, and read into it anything you like.

God has authority over nature because he created it. That's partly how Jesus' identity was confirmed to the disciples – even the wind and the waves obeyed him (Mk. 4:41). He has authority over us, because he created us. It doesn't mean that God is a tyrannical bully who laughs maniacally while playing chess with our lives. To the contrary, the good artist loves the thing he has made, because he has poured himself into his work.

Some modern artists expressed their deep hurt after a fire destroyed a large amount of their work stored in a warehouse in London. Although segments of the public found the destruction amusing, the artists themselves felt that they had lost part of themselves. Their art expressed their experiences and insights into life, and it was meant to be enjoyed by others. For them, its destruction was lamentable, tragic.

Like the artist, God desires creation's flourishing and enjoyment. His sense of ownership over creation is not possessiveness, but love. In the famous phrase of Abraham Kuyper, 'There is not a square inch in the whole domain of our human experience over which Christ, who is Sovereign over ALL, does not cry, "Mine!"' There is nowhere that the Creator does not roam and lovingly leave his artistic fingerprints. God looked at what he made, and called it good. We are good in that we are valuable to him and bear his image. He considers us worthy of his love.

But we are not good in that we are often unfaithful in our relationship with him. Unlike works of art we are not inanimate objects – despite evidence to the contrary in the forms found on sofas all over Britain during weekend football matches! We have been given will and responsibility, as gifts of consciousness. From Adam and Eve in the garden of Eden, to the present day, we betray the goodness in us when we seek to deny God's authority to guide our interpretation of life. We want life on our own terms. We don't want to read the instructions before we operate the appliance. We insist on the freedom to read into our lives whatever meaning we want, and miss P. T. Forsyth's point that we're only really free when we recognize that we're not free at all.

Part of God's love is the aspect of holiness. It is what makes his love good and perfect. It is the content that tells us what love will do, and what love will not do. Otherwise, how would we know love at all? Our rejection of God involves a rejection of his holiness and his instructions for good living. It affects the way we live, and the way we understand the world.

Our prideful rebellion against God marks all of our relationships. It has repercussions for how we relate to God, to one another, to the planet. And it runs the hopeless risk of self-destruction. We reject God's authority and take it upon ourselves. Our destruction of the physical environment is just one example of how we read into nature what we want, instead of what God wants.

God entrusted the creation to human stewardship. He told us to look after what he had made, to nurture it in order that it might flourish and nourish its inhabitants. In a breach of our relationship with God, humans became greedy, and found that they could exploit the creation for their own desires. The planet became a resource to tap rather than a garden to tend. Riches and power could flow to those who had the knowledge and ability to take advantage of the earth's treasures.

Some of us recognize this belief as a fallacy. The earth's resources are not endless, and its treasures are finite. There is enough to meet the needs of all, but we haven't taken seriously our mandate as stewards. The result is a planet that is poisoned beyond recovery, and an inequality of existence that is unjustifiable. In the west, we pollute the air as we consume more electricity and drive bigger cars. We drink up the natural resources of the planet and watch other humans die of thirst. No wonder we end up with a culture that has no sense of purpose or meaning.

Our rebellion against God, then, is more than just the sins that you and I commit on a daily basis. They are part of the picture, but they do not fill the frame. Our individual sins are compounded when we act as members of societies that jostle with one another for power to control the wealth that is made available by manipulating creation. Soon we think that our own cultures are gods, and that we have the right to exercise our own authority over the whole of nature, let alone our own lives. We sin against God, but we also sin against each other. We refuse to live out the implications of a healthy relationship with God (righteousness) in our relationships with each other (justice). The two are intimately connected.

The story of the fall of individuals is told through Adam and Eve, and the story of the collective fall is told through the tower of Babel in Genesis 11. The building of the tower is a story of collective pride, the sin of a people who wish to be like God, in the same way that Adam and Eve wanted to be like God. In collective form, the sin is multiplied, because the extent of what they were able to accomplish in rebellion against God was so much greater than what one individual was capable of. God had to scatter the people and confuse their language to prevent their collective pride from destroying them altogether. Even here, God's punishment is for their own good, and meted out not in simple retribution, but because he wants for them the best life possible.

Graciously, God doesn't just leave us to our destruction. There is a sense in which he allows us the freedom to pursue the destructive ends of our own desires (Rom. 1:18–25). But he wants us to acknowledge his authorship, and to enjoy the shalom, the wholeness, of our relationship with him, each other, and the whole earth. Even though we rebel as individuals, and as societies, he stoops to meet us, and woo us back to the good life.

Covenant v. the myth of creative distance

Who can resist the Bette Midler version of the song *From a Distance*? Even if you have no affinity for the Cliff Richard take on the single, you can't help but sing along and even be moved by the sentiments it contains. From a distance, the world is beautiful, colourful, and at peace. There is a sense that God sits back, and looks at the earth from a distance, and watches. But that's it. There's no consideration of how God reacts, or what he might think or do in response to our warlike activities. Like the grand old man in the sky he just, well, watches. And maybe eats popcorn. It sounds more like entertainment than involvement.

The Bible gives us a very different picture of how God takes the initiative to relate to us, how he responds to our sinful behaviour, our rebellion against him, and our ill-treatment of one another. He's angry, but involved. He judges, but loves and woos. When we find ourselves in the wilderness, he's there. When we wander in the desert, we find he's wooed us there in order to speak softly to us, and bring us back to a place of trust and security. He punishes sin, but he'd rather not have to. He'd rather walk with us in the cool of the morning in the garden that he made and said was good.

Even though our sinful rebellion caused a fissure in our relationship with our Creator, he still desired to be involved with his creatures. By his grace – favour we do not deserve – he stayed involved with his world. Recognizing our abuse of the gift of freedom, God spelled out more specifically the parameters for our behaviour. Giving us the guidelines of law, he sought to protect us from our sinful inclinations that hurt ourselves and each other. And he didn't just want to watch us from a distance. Instead, he personally met with Abraham, and made a promise.

By making a promise to Abraham, God entered a covenant with a group of people he could relate to directly. The unfolding of the promise would take many generations but it would be fulfilled. We could not cross the breach in our friendship with God so he reached over and made a way for our sin to be forgiven, a way for our relationship with him to be restored. Not to be exclusive, God made for himself a people who would be a light to all the nations, that all of creation might be restored to him.

He who is awesome in power and might deserves our deepest reverence and respect, and yet he stoops to meet us right where we stand. And then he lifts us up so we can see him, and talk to him in true friendship where we know him, and are known by him.

HE WHO IS AWESOME IN POWER AND MIGHT DESERVES OUR DEEPEST REVERENCE AND RESPECT, AND YET HE STOOPS TO MEET US RIGHT WHERE WE STAND.

As a child growing up in Canada, I used to watch a warm and welcoming television show called *The Friendly Giant*. Each episode would open with the voice of the giant inviting us to come on over to the castle where he'd 'hurry on in through the back door, let down the drawbridge, and open the big front door for you'. The camera would bring us inside the castle where there was a chair for someone to sit in, one for two more to curl up in, and for someone who likes to rock, a rocking chair in the middle. We were invited then to 'Look up, look wayyyyy up.' There we saw him at eye level, where he'd visit with his animal friends, play songs, and tell us stories. He was big and awesome, but safe and secure. It was easy to forget he was a giant.

The God of the universe invites us to meet at his castle. He bridges the gap of our sin by letting the drawbridge down over the moat. He invites us inside to enjoy his company. It is safe and secure, warm and welcoming. Sometimes we even forget that he's God.

And so did the people of Israel. The people God made a covenant with kept forgetting who he was. They forgot his promises to them, and they forgot theirs to him. They constantly kept turning away from him, and he constantly kept following after them and drawing them back to himself.

Despite God's direct involvement in his world, many still forget his presence. They get through life by not thinking too hard about it, because when they do, they end up in confusion. Nick Hornby's book *How to be Good* reflects the inevitable result of forgetting God, and what happens with our own efforts to do what we think is right. The characters of the book get into a terrible muddle trying to do the right things in life. More than that, they struggle with trying to know what the right thing is in the first place. By the end of the book, the main character is together at last with her family, enjoying the fun and togetherness of everyday life. But she catches a glimpse out the window in the darkness, and realizes with a certain sadness that there's nothing out there.

Behave the right way, perform the right actions, and then do what you like, so long as you don't hurt anybody. It's a far-from-rigorous view of ethics. And it leads to an inevitable sense of meaninglessness. This can apply to God's people too. At the time of the prophets, they thought that they could go through the motions of what was required without being required to have a change of heart. It is difficult for us to love each other, let alone God, on our own strength, despite our best efforts. Our own moral courage is simply not enough. When the prophets gave voice to God's desire for mercy not sacrifice, it arose from the callous way in which sacrifice was being offered. As a reminder of the seriousness of sin, and God's judgement over sin, sacrifice fulfilled the law, but it also was a challenge to live life with mercy from then on. God's people were flouting that reality, sinning wilfully and sacrificing to cover it. If they lived their lives rightly and didn't sin, they didn't need to sacrifice. But they were unable to live the sinless life on their own strength. Because of God's grace, and his love, he provided a way out of this vicious and damning circle, once and for all. A more radical, more permanent personal involvement was required. And God paid the ultimate price.

Christ v. the myth of the good teacher

'Long time ago, in Bethlehem, so the Holy Bible say, Mary's boy child, Jesus Christ, was born on Christmas day.' So goes the song. A cartoon baby in a manger. A revolutionary liberator. A champion of the marginalized and oppressed. A rabbi. A rabble-rouser. A deluded maniac. The images of Jesus Christ in our culture range from the comical to the blasphemous.

So who was Jesus? Those of us who are Christians ought to be able to answer that question. But often, when we think about it, we're not sure where to start. Is he the Christ, the promised one? Was he just a good example of how people should live? Was he inspired by God, or was he God in human flesh? What can we affirm about him, and what things should we let go? There are a lot of Christians today who want to look at Jesus afresh and get rid of what they suggest are historical misunderstandings of who Jesus was. Certainly we want to reach as clear a picture of him as possible, but it is difficult to discern what things witness to Jesus' real identity in history, and which things are mere historical constructions. If we hold together biblical teaching about Jesus with those consistent beliefs the church has held about him since its inception, we may not have a perfect picture of him, but we can be confident that it gives us a clear enough glimpse of him that we'll recognize him when we see him face to face.

Have you ever set up a meeting with someone you've never seen before? It can be difficult and amusing. I once had to meet with a student from the Christian Union at my university. Although we spoke many times on the phone, we'd never actually met face to face. We arranged to have lunch at a café, and in true clandestine style, she told me she would be the one wearing a red flower on her lapel. Of course, I couldn't miss her even in a crowd. We laughed and greeted one another and had a splendid time together.

We may lack a complete picture of what Jesus was all about. But he has not left us without clues to his identity. When we know him personally, he shows us what he is like. He prepares us to recognize him when we meet him face to face. Like my friend with the rose on her lapel, we can be sure he gives us enough clues that we'll know him when we see him!

So what are some of the things we can affirm about who Jesus was and what Jesus did? We have many biblical pictures of him and his work. He is the awaited Messiah, the one prophesied to save his chosen people. He is the Son of Man and the Son of God, affirming his identification with humanity and divinity. He is the Saviour of the world, demonstrating that he is good news for everybody, not just a select bouquet of believers. He died to restore the whole cosmos to fullness in its Creator, and to reconcile humanity.

In his life and teaching he challenged the old authorities, and included those who had been excluded. As a great teacher, he had the ability to challenge and offend, to nurture and to grow the preconceived notions of those who listened to him. But he was more than a teacher. He was tempted in every way, and yet remained sinless. He showed us how to live and invited us to follow him, but where he went, we could not go. His journey to the cross was a lonely one, and yet, we all were there.

In the cross, Christ pays a ransom to redeem us; wins a victory over sin and death; takes what our sin deserves in our place; challenges the principalities and powers of darkness in this world. In the cross, Christ did something for us, and for God. He redeemed us from the punishment we were due, and vindicated God's holy love. He showed the extent of his love, as the work of the cross flowed from grace. What was once mystery has been revealed. Christ tasted death, and rose again so that we might have life and have it to the full.

> CHRIST TASTED DEATH, AND ROSE AGAIN SO THAT WE MIGHT HAVE LIFE AND HAVE IT TO THE FULL.

All of this stands against any notion that Jesus was simply a good teacher, or a positive example for living. The Bible and Christian history lead us beyond the Christ of the film *The Passion*. That portrayal of Jesus, for all of its accuracy, leaves us wondering *why* he suffered such cruel punishment. It appealed to many because we were left to draw our own conclusions from the art on the screen. Yet the Bible is clear about why Jesus suffered. He was wounded for our wilful rebellion and bruised for our lack of faithfulness. His whole life was lived in obedience to the Father. He had complete integrity in his mission. He also fulfilled the law and made us free from the bonds of law. By his grace we can taste the true freedom of obedience to him as we live life rightly related to him and each other today. In Christ we are more than creations. We are new creations. He takes the things in our lives that are a mess, and he makes them completely new.

Nobody but the promised Christ could fit such a description. Surely Jesus taught many good things that are worthy of attention and did many good things that are worthy of emulation. But he didn't merely *demonstrate* something through his life and work; he *did* something. He accomplished a way for our relationship with God to be restored once and for all. What we couldn't do for ourselves, he did for us. Truly this man was the Son of God.

Call v. the myth of hedonism

The philosopher Philip de Botton has recently identified
'status anxiety' as a significant characteristic of western
culture. This is the idea that we are overcome with stress
trying to keep up with the latest trends, coolest designs,
and simply the latest version of a given product. Most of us
can identify with this in at least a small way. The computer
you just bought six months ago is already struggling to
keep up with the software updates. It's obsolete by two
generations already. And you were so pleased to show it
off when it was new! The shine didn't last for long. You
feel destined to be the kind of person who lags behind in
everything. Oh, for just a moment of glory as the cool dude
on the block! Wait a minute – is that a new Land Rover?
Gotta get one of those!

The economist Robert Frank has called ours a 'winner-
take-all' society. He highlights the fact that the top 1 per
cent of people in British and American society control
more than 25 per cent of all wealth. The rich are getting
increasingly more rich, while the pay gap between top
earners and regular workers grows. The illusion is created
that all the world and his dog wears Armani and owns a
Gucci watch. Easily affordable to the rich, luxury consumer
products are sought by those who go into serious debt to
feel part of a hedonistic consumer culture. It is an absurd
situation.

As Christians, we too live in this culture. We are influenced by the constant demands of advertising that insist
we need things we didn't even know existed. We want to
keep up with the trends, we don't want to be left behind.
Even if not for ourselves, we know that it is important for
our children to wear the right brand names. It's not just a
matter of not depriving them, but a matter of safety. Kids
who wear the wrong brands get bullied, and those who

wear the ones that are too expensive get beaten up and have them stolen.

We do not have to crumble under the pressure this creates. But it is easy to become disoriented, and forget what our purpose in life is. Is the point of life to have all the right possessions, to be successful in the eyes of the world, or is it simply to put in time until Jesus comes again? We are not only creatures in relationship with our God, but we are people who are called with a purpose in this world. After the resurrection, Jesus ascended to the Father. There he intercedes for us as we carry out his mission in this world. The Spirit empowers, comforts, motivates and convicts as we journey in this world as pilgrims with a destination.

The sociologist Zygmunt Bauman talks about how some people wander through contemporary life like tourists, or vagabonds. They have no sense of orientation, and wander without meaning, or simply seek the next exciting thrill. The growing pastime of shopping as family entertainment, the proliferation of adventure holidays, and the demand for increasingly individualized products and services in our culture affirms the notion that we seem to live without significant purpose. Well, except for the purpose to accumulate. We line up goods

WE LINE UP GOODS AND EXPERIENCES LIKE TROPHIES ON A SHELF. WE HAVE TOP 10 LISTS OF PLACES WE MUST VISIT, RESTAURANTS WE MUST TRY, MOUNTAINS WE MUST CLIMB, BANDS WE MUST SEE. WE CHECK THEM OFF AS THOUGH BY EXPERIENCING THEM, WE POSSESS THEM. THE UNCEASING SEARCH FOR PLEASURE PERPETUATES THE MYTH OF HEDONISM IN THE CONTEMPORARY WORLD.

and experiences like trophies on a shelf. We have top 10 lists of places we must visit, restaurants we must try, mountains we must climb, bands we must see. We check them off as though by experiencing them, we possess them. The unceasing search for pleasure perpetuates the myth of hedonism in the contemporary world.

A biblical view of life challenges this myth at its core. Our purpose in life as Christians is clear, 'Go and make disciples of all nations, baptizing them in the name of the Father, and of the Son and of the Holy Spirit, and teach them to obey everything I have commanded you.' 'Love the Lord your God with all your heart, soul, mind, and strength, and love your neighbour as yourself.' Our purpose in life is vocational, that is, regardless of our particular circumstances or jobs, we have a call from God to live our lives in ways that honour him minute by minute and day by day. We may enjoy life, but we enjoy it because we recognize the gift of life from him. We know it in its fullness because of Christ. We accept work as part of our calling, and not simply something to be tolerated as a means of supporting the things we *really* want to do, or a way to get the things we *really* want to have.

Our call is simple – to love God, others, and ourselves, and to look after the gift of creation. That gives direction to everything else in our lives. But there is also distinctive content to our call. Because we love God and others, we are sent to make disciples. We can only make disciples if we are disciples. We can never lead people where we've never gone before.

In order to be and to make disciples, we have to recognize that there is a cost to being a Christian in today's world. We must be willing to carry our cross, die to self and our own desires, and be radically transformed by the Spirit of God. This means having our worldview – the way we organize our thoughts about the world in which we live

– reordered by the Spirit. Paul puts it this way, 'Therefore, I urge you, brothers and sisters, in view of God's mercy, to offer your bodies as living sacrifices, holy and pleasing to God. This is your spiritual act of worship. Do not conform any longer to the pattern of the world, but be transformed by the renewing of your mind. Then you will be able to test and approve what God's will is – his good, pleasing and perfect will' (Rom. 12).

As we surrender our desires to own, possess, experience, and accumulate, we can have our worldview reordered. Through the disciplines of the spiritual life – prayer, Bible study, worship, shared community, love in action – we feed our mind, and our actions, so that we more closely begin to reveal the image of Christ in us.

Moreover, we are built into a community that shares this task together in the world. As God's people together, we witness to a different way of living that rejects the myth of hedonism, and embraces the call of God on our lives. Together we worship and share the joys and challenges of what it means to worship God, and serve the world as the body of Christ, broken and spilled out. We can rethink, rework, rebuild what it means to be church today, but it always comes back to this: If we are anything but a body of disciples making disciples, serving God and others with Christ's love, we are not the church for today. In all of our striving, we risk losing our sense of discipleship. If we're not disciples, we're not a church, but just a group of hedonists gelling around some nebulous spirituality.

It's not what we do but what God does in us that will last. Being a community is a gift from God that builds the most unlikely companions together into a household of faith. It's not always an easy path to follow, but it's the only path for followers of 'the way'. And so we follow his voice as it calls – until he comes again.

Consummation v. the myth of meaninglessness

Nihilism is everywhere these days. Suddenly it's almost fashionable to believe that everything comes to nothing, and nothing means anything. The American television show *Six Feet Under* which I would recommend only to the most hardened Christian culture vultures, emphasizes the theme of nihilism to the extreme. The opening credits alone paint a powerful picture of the worldview that everything comes to nothing, eventually. Every episode opens with death, and ends by emphasizing the isolation and emptiness of life. The characters find little consolation in relationships and activities. In the end, everything is hollow, and death has the last word.

Similar notions are communicated through the art of Mark Rothko. An existentialist painter seeking ever purer form of colour and style, Rothko's personal isolation grew as his art developed. In a room of great ethereal blocks of black and red at the Tate Modern, we can share some of the beauty and despair the artist encountered. We may be left feeling understood, but also uninspired. The work cannot point beyond itself to anything else. There is nothing more to see. We are not surprised to learn that Rothko committed suicide, nor are we surprised that his art is immensely popular at this moment in our culture. Nihilism seems to rule the day.

Even those who resist this negative take on life find it difficult to put something meaningful in its place. Perhaps meaning is to be found in family. But wait, families are broken down all over the place. We don't even know what family is any more. Maybe meaning can be found in our friendships. But that can only take us so far. Perhaps we can find meaning in shopping, or work. At the end of a Friday night we may still be left wondering what it's all about. Better not to think about it – party the night away.

Many people avoid thinking about meaning at all. It's too dangerous, too scary to go down that road of asking whether our lives have any significance. Better to take control of the fear that they might not, by accumulating wealth and belongings, or hide behind a convenient spirituality where we can have a spa weekend and meet with God on our own terms. Maybe the concept of meaning doesn't really mean anything and we're seeking after an ideal.

A biblical view of what happens in the end contradicts a nihilist interpretation of life. We live as a people in waiting, as we keep our lamps burning in anticipation of Christ's return. Then, the whole of creation that has been groaning in eager anticipation will find its fulfilment, the kingdom will come in its fullness, and we will see Christ face to face. This is the real hope that challenges our sense of meaninglessness in this world. It assures us that there is a point to life, and our lives make a difference within the unfolding of God's work in creation. We live our lives now in view of the hopeful and inspiring glimpse we get of the future to come.

This is a great relief to most of us: the coming of God's kingdom doesn't depend on us 'getting it all right', but is a gift that comes to us and through us, from him.

YES OUR LIVES ARE IMPORTANT, AND THE THINGS WE DO ARE MEANINGFUL. BUT THE WHOLE CHRISTIAN PROJECT WON'T COLLAPSE IF WE'RE LESS THAN PERFECT.

Yes our lives are important, and the things we do are meaningful. But the whole Christian project won't collapse if we're less than perfect. Like the best dinner parties, people will eat and enjoy themselves, even if we burn the appetizers and the soufflés don't rise to their full height. At the same time, we will have a sense that what we've committed ourselves to is worthwhile, in fact, it's the real stuff of life.

And so these are some of the main ingredients on which we base our cooking in the contemporary world. These are the familiar ingredients that determine the overall nature of the recipes we will devise. They all need to be held together in proper balance, for fully-orbed flavour. If one dominates, it can overpower the others, rather than bring out the best in them. For example, if you emphasize creation, you might forget the fall and have no need of a saviour. If you emphasize consummation, you might always be waiting for the end, and forget the importance of living life to the full in the here and now. There is room for some degree of diversity in the recipes we come up with, but the main ingredients need to be present in greater or lesser degree.

If these are the 'store cupboard' ingredients of Christian faith, what are the seasonal ingredients with which they have to be combined? What is the next stage in assembling our feast?

2

Assembling the Ingredients: Seasonal Produce

Assembling the Ingredients: Seasonal Produce

Tension in a world of contrasts

Feeling tense? Our world today is full of paradoxes: contradictions that make our lives feel insecure, and our identities fragile. Like oil and water that simply don't mix, our culture is changing in one direction that pushes us to change in another. We feel out of step with each other, with God, with ourselves. Some people say nothing endures but change. Others chant with the pop group The Talking Heads and say, 'Same as it ever was.' In some ways, that's true. But in a relatively short period of time much has changed. In our own lifetime, technology has doubled, trebled, and over again. We have a sense that looking out of the church window gives us a very different view on the world than we would have had a generation ago.

Many of the changes that have taken place in our culture over the past 50 or 100 years have led us to feel out of sync with the world around us. Although we are very much part of the culture, and it contributes to our understanding of ourselves, our lives as individuals often feel in tension with the bigger picture. So what exactly has changed? How is our view different, and what has it done to the way we feel about the world in which we live?

These are the seasonal ingredients of the environment that surrounds us, and through which we look at the world. They change over time, and have a transient nature. They influence us, and we have the opportunity to influence them. We need to be familiar with these ingredients, special for today, so we know what it is that we will later have to combine with our stock ingredients.

TENSION 1

The world has become smaller

Remember when it seemed exotic to have a holiday abroad? Or how exciting it was to receive a letter from some distant land with its strange animal stamp in the corner? No? I'm not surprised. It's been a long time since such occurrences were anything but commonplace. A holiday abroad now is considered a right. Many people feel cheated if they don't get two per year. And each day we correspond with people all over the world via the internet.

Once upon a time, if someone committed to a life of missionary service, they could expect to travel for weeks to arrive at their destination and not return home until their period of service was over. If a loved one was ill or died, there was no expectation of a quick visit home. Letters took months to arrive at their destination. Considering the performance of the Royal Mail sometimes, it still may seem like months! But in reality, we can get anywhere in the world in a matter of hours, and contact anywhere in the world in a matter of seconds. Suddenly, our big, exciting, exotic world seems rather small. And we stomp our feet if our five-hour flight across the ocean is delayed for an hour.

This reality has brought change to our travel and communication habits abroad, and also to our communities at home. Increased mobility has brought the richness of diversity to our neighbourhoods, such that the world is now in our sitting rooms. We don't have to go far to relate to people of various cultures. They are our neighbours, co-workers, friends, and family.

It used to be that people would ask someone they met from Toronto, 'Do you know Joe? He's from Canada.' Such a question was usually an indicator that the person had relatively few contacts with Canadians, and misunderstood the geography involved. Most of us would laugh at the question. But I don't laugh so much any more. Increased communications around the world mean that I now goad people who say they know someone in Canada to ask me if I know them. You'd be surprised how many times we strike gold.

The world has truly become a small place.

My world's become bigger

At the same time that the world has become smaller, it seems that our individual worlds have grown infinitely larger. At one time, most people would grow up, work, and live in communities within close proximity to their birthplace. Career choices were limited by circumstances of birth and privilege, gender and resources. A holiday abroad was a once-in-a-lifetime event, earned after years of work and saving.

Today, our days are filled with choices and decisions that leave us almost paralysed. Should I do this job or that one? Should I live in this country or somewhere else? Will I travel to Malta or Cyprus, Malaysia or Vietnam? The options before us are infinite. We feel a great tension as we live within the paradox that this small world seems so big to us. We have little control over far-off events that affect our lives. We become confused about who we are and where we're going. The smaller the world becomes, the bigger it feels to us as individuals. Sometimes we're simply overwhelmed.

Today the news broadcasts fill our sitting rooms with a world at our fingertips, but it all seems so out of control. It may be small, but its problems feel boundless. Too big to handle, sometimes.

TENSION 2

The world has become more homogenous

Television has brought the world together. We may not like the fact that advertising through the mass media means that Coca-Cola and the golden arches are among the most recognized symbols in the world. But it is a fact nonetheless. Wherever communication opens up, television goes. Wherever television goes, markets are paved through advertising. Wherever markets open up, cultures are converted into consumer products, and the world becomes remarkably the same.

If you were to parachute into the centre of several major cities in the world, and you were not too traumatized by the experience, you would discover incredible similarities between them. In many cases, you might be hard pressed to recognize what country you were in. I thought it was amusing to hear of the Korean boy at a Scout Jamboree in Chicago marvel how the burgers there tasted just like the ones in Seoul.

Languages, customs, and cultures still have distinctions, to be sure. But they are not as sharp as they used to be. There is a global culture forming through international markets and communication. Increasingly, we dress the same, speak the same language, desire the same future for ourselves and our children. How shocked we are when we encounter people whose dream is quite unlike our own.

My world's become more diverse

At the same time as global markets are perpetuating a certain cultural sameness in the world, we find that our world as individuals feels so much more diverse than ever before. The same markets that impose homogeneity across cultures bring diversity to those with the resources to pay.

We are provided with a rich diversity even as we consume cultures around us. We're happy to have a Buddha in the hallway and a Mayan tapestry on the wall in the living room. Cultural symbols from other lands become the kitsch of our interior décor, eclectically assembled to display our sophistication, and our willingness to engage with difference.

An Indian takeaway tonight, a Chinese buffet tomorrow, mangetout from Zaire and asparagus from Peru the next day. We are surrounded by the sights, sounds, and smells of diversity. We welcome the stranger, and invite him to be our friend. We have a sense that our lives are made better because of this diversity. And yet, we are still uncomfortable. What does it mean to be me in the midst of this cultural milieu?

There is a tension between this positive attitude towards diversity and the fact of cultural homogenization. Does the diversity I experience come at a price to someone else? Is it real? Is the diversity that enriches my life built on an imposed sameness somewhere else? We are haunted by the thought that the benefits of diversity are consumed only by those who have enough money to buy the dream that we thought we all shared. And we are forced to recognize that much of the diversity we experience is artificial, leaving us uncertain as to who we are in the midst of shifting sand.

TENSION 3

The world has become more connected

Think for a minute about how many connections you have with people and places around the world. You may be connected through your business, or work. Perhaps you have connections through your school or college. Maybe you have friends or family who live in various places. Perhaps you have a special relationship with a church somewhere, through your own church at home. Maybe your town is twinned with another, or several others. How many can you come up with?

Think also about the ways that you are connected. Perhaps you visit. You probably use email, maybe even with a webcam. You may use snail mail, and phonecalls, newsletters, couriers, and so on. It's incredible, isn't it?

Now think about the various ways we are connected to our workplace, our friends, and our families closer to home. We communicate through the internet, through mobile phones, wirelessly and easily. We text, email, voicemail, videophone. All of this has become central to our lives in just a few short years.

The advantages are obvious. Through the internet, the voiceless can suddenly have a voice. Those whose cause was unheard-of, can have their concerns brought to the attention of the world. Campaigns can be organized, and networks used to facilitate action on issues of common concern. For our everyday lives, we simply are grateful for the convenience of communication, and the peace of mind that comes with knowing our loved ones are always just a text message away.

My world's become more alienated

We are connected in more ways than ever before. Yet, for all of these technological advances, we are remarkably isolated and lonely people. When Sarah woke up this morning there were 12 emails waiting for her. Eight were spam, two were jokes forwarded from friends but without any personal message. One was from Asia, and one from South America. She heard her phone beep, and found a text message from a friend. She responded. She went out, got some money from a bank machine, and bought some milk and bread without even noticing the shopkeeper. She went home, surfed the net for a while, updated her blog (with guilt because she'd been neglecting it), watched TV and went to bed, where she cried herself to sleep. She'd been in touch with many people, from all over the world in just a few hours. The lives of many people touched her own. But she never shared a smile with a neighbour let alone enjoy a meaningful conversation with another human being. No wonder she's lonely. No wonder we are.

We have the means to communicate more, faster, further than ever before. But the technology is not neutral. In its structure it is individualistic, and designed for consumption rather than real human communication. Computers are made for one person using one keyboard, looking at one screen. Mobile phones are increasingly designed for one person to access information rather than communicate directly with another human being. We have to work hard against these tendencies in order for technology to really help us connect with other people, and not just serve individualistic ends. And what about the people who cannot afford to own the technology that allows them to participate in a highly networked society? They are potentially excluded from this new world. The very technology that can give them a voice leaves them isolated and marginalized in their poverty or oppression.

It should come as no surprise that we have surrendered to the new cultural phenomenon of flash mobbing, where individuals find a sense of community in the bizarre. The first flash mob in London took place in a furniture store, where people gathered via a pub, after following initial instructions on the internet. They were all told to gather at the shop, stroke and admire the sofas, and make a mobile phone-call without using the letter 'o'. After 10 minutes everybody went home. More recently there was a brief pillow fight outside of St Paul's. It's a bit of harmless fun, and an attempt to express community in a technologically sophisticated and alienating world.

> THE WORLD IS HIGHLY CONNECTED. YET, TOO OFTEN, WE LOOK AT EACH OTHER AND SEE ONLY STRANGERS.

The world is highly connected. Yet, too often, we look at each other and see only strangers.

TENSION 4

The world is progressing

Despite a great popular wave of disenchantment with the myth of secular progress, our culture is actually advancing in many ways. Concern for the marginalized in society is expressed, at least to some degree, by most people. Although our social welfare system has struggled to pay its way in some respects, there is little question that some sort of safety net is appropriate. The provision of universal health care, and means of avoiding extreme poverty, are principles to which our society is largely committed. This may be a fact that many of us take for granted, and we often complain that social provision could be better executed, but those who benefit from social assistance would have endured a dire life by comparison had they lived a hundred years ago.

In the realm of science and technology, we have seen perhaps the most drastic advances of progress in recent years. The genetic code has been cracked, new cures and treatments for disease have been pioneered, and global communication is more efficient than ever before in history. This is not a merely remote reality, but a present one that affects our daily lives. Need surgery? Keyhole techniques so reduce your recovery time that you're likely to go home the next day rather than stay in hospital for weeks.

Digital television allows us to interact with the action on our screens. Access to the internet puts information and services at our fingertips that we never dreamed possible. Childless couples have infinite choices to make about the type of fertility treatment they might pursue. Need to get somewhere? Check out the map on the internet, and key into traffic reports for your route as you drive – all through your mobile phone. Better still, get a satellite navigation system for your car. The rapid advance of scientific discovery almost defies our human ability to keep up in terms of reflection: Does it promote or compromise a healthy life for the benefit of all?

In recent days in our culture, we are also witnessing increasing concern for levels of global inequality. Unlike the character Gecko from the film *Wall Street*, most of us find it difficult to agree that unfettered 'greed is good'. The sense of responsibility that comes with success may simply reflect contemporary guilt in the face of increasing knowledge about how most of the world lives. But the growing commitment to fair trade, and to protest against injustice, reveal a society that possesses at least the potential to improve. With will and commitment as a society, we possess the potential to progress at a dizzyingly rapid rate.

Perhaps the best word to use is opportunity. The progress that our world is seeing still largely benefits a few, and we are often unsure what to do with what we've learned. But with the advances we are seeing comes immense opportunity to progress in many positive directions. An end to some diseases, access to education, potential to tackle poverty, are all opportunities that lie before us.

My **world's paralysed by choice**

There's no question that the advances we have seen in science and technology, and in production and marketing, have left us with more choices in life than most of us can handle. This was brought home to me in a very simple way soon after I moved to Britain from Canada. Previously, I could do my weekly grocery shop in record time. I had sussed out the products I liked, and knew just where they were located in the supermarket. I could spin my trolley through the store and be on my way in a few well-timed minutes. When I did my first shop after moving, it seemed as though it took all day. It began when I stood in front of the margarine cooler and was faced with a wall of a hundred brands of spread. With butter, without butter, with olive oil, spreadable, reduced fat, good for cooking. I had to look at them all in order to decide which one I should buy. I was almost paralysed by choice. I finally made a decision and moved on. Then it started all over again when I hit the muesli shelf.

This degree of choice hits us everywhere we turn. Over 100,000 books were published in Britain this year. Which ones will you choose to read? New films are released every week. Which ones will you see? Can't decide what to watch on TV tonight? Why not tape the show you don't watch? Admit it – you've got a shelf of unwatched tapes, full of programmes you'll never see. Better watch them fast because they're not selling VCRs any more. Some future-watchers think that even DVDs will bite the dust before the decade is out. So, will you select a DVD+R or DVD-R? Recordable or play only? Or just forget the DVD altogether and opt for recordable hard disk?

Some of our choices are more serious. They raise even more challenging questions. Should Grandma's life support be turned off? Perhaps the new stem cell research will offer her a cure. Wait a minute – is stem cell research morally right? Should we benefit from genetic engineering and aborted foetuses? When we're faced with the choices that involve matters of life and death, things become far more confusing. Often, we're prevented from action because we are faced with so many facets of choice, we simply don't know what to do. Laws are enacted that affect all of our society and there is little input from a Christian point of view because we honestly don't know what to think, let alone what to say.

Sometimes it just doesn't feel like progress at all.

TENSION 5

The world is safe

Do you remember the Doomsday Clock? It's the popular device that global strategists used in the 1980s to measure how close we were to the end of the world. At the beginning of the decade, it was set at 3 minutes to midnight – the end of the world was nigh. Through environmental degradation, and the potential for all-out nuclear destruction, it looked as though we wouldn't be around for long. At the worst point late in the Cold War, the clock was set to one minute to midnight. A generation grew up in the shadow of a mushroom cloud, and every night we wondered if we would wake up to another day.

Then the unthinkable happened. When the Berlin Wall came down, the world changed almost overnight. Programmes to dismantle the missiles that had been aimed for self-destruction moved into overdrive, and for the first time in history, nations not only ceased nuclear weapons production, but destroyed weapons already deployed. For the first time in decades, the hands on the Doomsday Clock moved backwards, and our fear that we would annihilate the earth in a single weapons exchange faded away.

Peace came to diverse places where Cold War skirmishes had been played out away from the western gaze. Within a short period of time, numerous wars found resolution. Depending on where in the world you found yourself, things started to look better. We seemed to enter an unprecedented period of stability. Some people benefited enormously, while others were simply forgotten.

My world's more dangerous

For a while we all felt rather secure. Maybe even smug. We took security for granted. But on September 11, 2001, everything changed. For some people, in some parts of the world, of course, those events were given only a sideways glance. Their security, their daily survival had long been under threat. But this was a first for the western world – a hit on American soil. This went against the grain of how North Americans viewed the world. The myth of living in 'the fireproof house' was destroyed. Conflicts happen elsewhere, but not in our land. Such a symbolic hit was going to demand unique retribution. We still don't know fully what it will mean for our future. But we feel much more afraid personally, on a daily basis, than we used to. The fact that the emotional appeal to security played so significantly in the American presidential elections of 2004 is reflective of how insecure we have become. And the theme hasn't yet finished running its course on the European side of the ocean.

It's your morning trip to work on the underground. You glance around at your fellow passengers with gnawing suspicion. What's she hiding under her coat? Why is she fidgeting nervously? What's in her bag? The thought of a nuclear bomb flying in from some superpower doesn't even cross your mind. But maybe today is the day the dirty

> BUT MAYBE TODAY IS THE DAY THE DIRTY BOMB HITS *YOUR* TRAIN, IN *YOUR* NEIGHBOURHOOD.

bomb hits *your* train, in *your* neighbourhood. Barely a day has passed in three years that you haven't thought about the planes that fly over your office tower as you work. And admit it. You have several bottles of water, a crate of tinned beans, and an emergency radio stored away in your garage. Just in case.

The sociologist Zygmunt Bauman identified the growing insecurity in our culture long before the attacks of September 11. In his book *In Search of Politics,* he considered how western society has changed in recent decades. Rapid mobility and changes in the way we relate to one another in communities have left us fearful, uncertain, and insecure. If Bauman is right, then recent fragmented acts of terrorism have only served to reinforce our fear and isolation as we trade stable communities of trust for close networks of common interest. Our sense of insecurity becomes a preoccupation with fear and leaves us with little interest in the places of the world where the experience of life is truly insecure. Many countries and people manipulated by the superpowers during the Cold War are now largely left out in the cold. It's hard to share the gospel through a door that's shut and bolted.

So what does all of this mean for how our culture views the world? It is essential that we understand the nature of these changing ingredients if we are to balance them properly with the traditional ingredients of the good news, both in our own lives and for others. Let's take a look at how our culture has flowed through the past two or three generations. This will involve drawing out some broad generalizations. But hopefully that will give us some clues as to how we got here from there, and where we might be headed next. Too often, the church lags behind in its understanding of the culture in which we live and of which we are part. Understanding the trends will give us some clues as to what our discipleship and evangelism might look like in this strange new world.

How we got here from there

THE WORLD OF MY GRANDMA

My grandmother grew up in a town where everybody knew her name. They knew where she was born, who her parents were, and what she did with her time. She lived, married, raised children, worked and died in that town. I think she was pretty typical of her generation. Except for a few wealthy or particularly adventurous types in search of a more exotic experience, most people tended to have few choices about their lives. Women married and had children, or possibly ventured into a career in nursing or education, but certainly not both. Men had more choice, but even theirs was limited by family circumstance and education. Usually, they carried on in a career not unlike that of some relative. Except for demands of the war, few ventured far afield.

My grandmother would never have asked herself, 'Who am I?' If I had asked her that question, she'd have thought I was playing a game. This is not to say that she wasn't self-reflective, rather that her self-reflection usually focused on the limited choices she had about her life, the things that she did, and the way others treated her rather than who she was, in herself. She was more interested in asking survival questions, like, 'How will I pay the bills?' and 'How can I make sure my children have a better life than mine?'

This gave her life a certain sense of direction. She knew that through education and good nurturing, she could expect progress from generation to generation. Her sense of purpose in life derived in part from labouring to ensure that life would be easier and more enjoyable for her children, and grandchildren. Where was she going? Home from her job at the bakery to chop firewood and cook supper so that her children could study. Hers was a very practical and community-focused existence, and a relatively hard life. But she looked after her neighbours when they were ill, and sent cakes on special occasions. She always had time for a chat. And we always knew when we visited her that there would be something delicious on the stove, and a good laugh waiting in the kitchen.

Her sense of truth was very practical. God, values, family and friends were true. She didn't think about how she knew that. Or whether they were philosophical figments of her imagination. She wasn't a committed Christian until very late in life, but she never doubted that God existed. She knew for certain the things that she could see, and the things that were handed to her by tradition. I remember one day that she had an argument with my grandfather over something she had seen in the paper. Neither of them believed anything until they saw it 'in black and white'. My grandfather doubted the facts of what she was telling him, but they both knew it would be settled if she could find the original news item. The heated discussion was over when she found the paper and showed him something in print. If it was printed in the paper, it must be true.

This was reflective of the wider culture at the time. Remember the story *Yes Virginia, there is a Santa Claus*? A little girl named Virginia doubted whether Father Christmas was real. Her father assured her that 'if you see it in The *Sun*, it's so'. She wrote to the newspaper to determine whether, in fact, Santa was real. The printing of the editor's reply brought closure to the matter as she was assured that there was indeed a Santa Claus. We are too aware of hidden agendas, spin tactics, and political affiliations for such simple belief in the printed word to take on the same authority in life today. Time and circumstance have made us necessarily sceptical, and sadly cynical.

Because my grandmother's existence was so parochial, the world was a very big place indeed. In her 85 years, she never flew on a plane, and had never been off the continent of North America. Far away places were distant and exotic. In many ways, they were strangely irrelevant. Diversity was suspect because it was unfamiliar. Why concern yourself with issues that aren't staring you in the face? The war demanded that men and women travel abroad to defend the ideals they held dear. But the goal was always to get back home to where you once belonged. Only, as Heraclitus recognized, there is no going back. You really cannot step into the same river twice. Nothing after the war could be the same again. In the ensuing years, the world began to get a lot smaller.

THE WORLD OF MY MUM

Everything's groovy. You've got flowers in your hair, and more beads than brain cells after all those substances you experimented with. Sorry, I forgot. You didn't inhale. The post-war baby boom generation was energetic, experimental, and idealistic. People enjoyed new freedom through the sexual revolution spawned by advances in birth control methods. Social and economic recovery after the war gave them unprecedented opportunities for trying out various relationships, jobs, and ideas. Liberation movements sprang up and revolution was in the air. In time, many from that generation matured and took advantage of the opportunities given them by parents who had sacrificed for the benefit of their children. They were successful, worldly, and accrued and generated great wealth. Theirs was a generation considered to enjoy a quality of life far greater than their parents.

But they were not content with what they achieved. This was the world of my mum.

My mum left her hometown as soon as she was old enough. She forged a path towards a new identity in a city where she knew only one or two people. She trained for a career before she got married, which was crucial because she needed to fall back on it when my parents divorced and she was forced to raise her children on her own. But unlike my grandparents, who had to go to work at a young age, she'd had a few years of fun as a single young woman before settling down into 'real life'. She had an increased number of choices to make about her life, as she encountered numerous alternatives about children, community, and lifestyle.

Increased mobility, fragmented communication, diverse communities, and numerous lifestyle choices produced a generation of self-reflective individuals who weren't sure about their identity. The question 'Who am I?' was asked with greater frequency, and we witnessed the emergence of a therapy culture. With a rejection of traditional values, answers to life's problems were not often found in drugs or science, or in God and family. Answers had to be found within. It wasn't as easy as taking a tablet for a headache. These problems demanded more 'complex' solutions.

Truth was not something that was self-evident. It was more a journey of discovery. Truth was the ideal of freedom. But freedom was so hard to come by, and so were the ideals. As it became increasingly clear that the revolution wasn't going to happen, we found our culture dominated by a group of people who were disillusioned, disappointed, disoriented, and wondering if they had sold out the ideals of political progress and social revolution for the good life.

While our society wallowed in a crisis of self-identity, bankruptcy of moral values, and uncertainty about what was real and good and true, the beginnings of a different kind of revolution were taking shape. Those who had taken on the challenge of building financial empires were recognizing the significance of emerging global markets. Some took full advantage of cheap labour, and open markets, while others bemoaned the exploitation of vulnerable communities. Many were happy to profit from the global situation, but others suspected we were sowing the seeds of future destruction for some, if the world was becoming increasingly interconnected.

Postwar immigration brought diverse cultures into regular contact in the modern western world for the first time. Cheap holidays abroad, international flights, and improved communications systems made cross-cultural contact a distinct possibility for many. It wasn't much, but there was a sense that the sombreros and stuffed broncos were only the beginning of a world to be conquered. Exotic, maybe not. But it brought some colour to grey Britain.

MY WORLD . . . AND BEYOND

Culture's become so fragmented, that there are too many social groups at school these days to even keep count. There are still a few cultural icons that most people key into, but there are so many TV channels, radio stations, internet sites, that our shared culture has really come under fire. This is the generation where gaming, MP3s, and Friday night culture come into their own.

Young people of this generation have more freedom than ever before, and the spending power to make it count. Drugs, expensive entertainment systems, alcohol and sex are all a present reality. It's the world of the iPod, the rave, the game cube, the brand name. The vast majority of kids have grown up with a television in the bedroom, and a computer at hand. There is little that seems out of reach.

Except for family stability, that is. Many people have come of age in a family that would have been described as dysfunctional, except that dysfunctionality is now the norm. Children conceived by sperm donation seek their biological fathers, even as some siblings come to terms with the fact that they all have different dads. Friendship groups begin to take priority over families as the main source of identity and support.

This generation has grown up with the reality of diversity. Religious education has included celebrations of Diwali and Eid, along with Christmas and Easter. Truth is a very fuzzy concept, and is completely relative. It's not just a matter that truth is mysterious, but it is so mysterious that we may as well each invent our own. Truth may exist, but we can only really guess at its meaning. This generation is willing to experiment with the spiritual meaning of life, but on their own terms.

The world itself is a place to be discovered. Many young people think nothing of a long gap-year adventure overseas. They will also expect holidays abroad during their education, and throughout their lives. The more exotic the destination, and the further away it is, the more appealing it will be. The paradox is that there are now few places left unspoiled by western tourism, and the ravages of commercial globalization. The markets opened up by the previous generation are now entrenched in nearly every part of the world. There is hardly a village untouched by western commercial interests.

This idea is captured well in the film *The Beach*, where Leonardo Di Caprio's character is a backpacker in search of the ultimate rare experience. Through word of mouth and cryptic clues, only the real backpacker – not the tacky tourist – is able to find the last paradise. Uncovering a gem not yet discovered by the outside world, finding the Beach is like arriving in Shangri-La. But even there, things are not really perfect. No matter where the backpacker goes, his identity shape-shifts around the priorities of others, leaving him hanging over the brink of their madness. Even at the end of his journey, after his return to 'the real world', our hero finds that his identity is a transient mystery.

MANY PEOPLE GENUINELY DO NOT KNOW WHO THEY ARE, OR WHO THEY ARE SUPPOSED TO BE.

Not surprisingly, identity has become a completely fluid concept for many in the contemporary world. By changing a set of clothes, and social context, we become anyone we want to be. We are one person at church, another in the pub, another at home, another at school or work. It is difficult to be able to answer the question, 'Who am I?' and it causes great anxiety. Rates of depression among adolescents and young adults have reached epidemic proportions. Many people genuinely do not know who they are, or who they are supposed to be.

The search for identity opens up many creative possibilities and opportunities. This generation is willing to explore the tough questions of life, and be real with each other. People are happy to express their emotions and experience of life and of God through music, art, poetry, and drama. They are much more suspicious of authority, and seek out shared leadership. However, they don't always respond well to commitment outside of a small friendship group.

These, then, are today's seasonal ingredients we have been given to use in our recipes. We cannot simply say that culture looks this way, or that way. In fact, we have people who represent all of these cultural trends in our churches and communities. Most of us embody a blend of more than one flavour.

The temptation in devising recipes is to seek out the ever new to meet the demands of the contemporary world. But the experiment with new-taste Coke a few years back encourages us to be careful to jump on the latest bandwagon simply because it's new. After all, every bandwagon eventually goes past, and we don't want to be stuck on it when it does. The newest is not necessarily the truest. And new-taste Coke was landed in the bin when the public decided that there was nothing wrong with the old Coca-Cola, now renamed, Coke Classic. Sometimes, despite the choice it offers us, a good old recipe is still the best.

So before we make any hasty decisions, one way or another, about what we will serve at our feast, we have to balance a few more considerations about how we will combine our traditional and seasonal ingredients without getting lost in our culture completely.

3

Ready Steady Cook

3

Ready Steady Cook

What's in the kitchen?

My favourite episodes of *Ready Steady Cook* (*Ready Set Cook* in North America) include those where the two competing chefs have exactly the same ingredients in the shopping bag. It is amazing to see what diverse dishes they will create from just a few simple ingredients, without bearing any similarity to one another whatsoever. For example, one day there was sirloin steak, brie, potato, red pepper, red onion and spinach in the bag.

The celebrity chef James Martin produced a mouth-watering red pepper soup with parsley pesto and brie croutes; herb crusted steak with spinach dauphinoise, patatas bravas, and egg Florentine – and all in 20 minutes! His rival Leslie Waters provided a tempting peppered cheese bruschetta with red pepper and orange chutney, a steak burger with Cajun chips and spinach mayonnaise, and an orange and spinach salad. Delicious.

If you are observant, and have never seen the show, you might well be wondering about the eggs and oranges. Where did *they* come from? Surely the chefs are not so creative as to be able to invent citrus fruit out of steak and spinach! Well, in addition to the ingredients in the shopping bag, the chefs have several store cupboard ingredients that are always available, such as eggs, milk, oranges, flour, sugar, herbs, and so on. These ingredients are given; they are available regardless of what the contestants might show up with in the shopping bag. They are standard ingredients without which few chefs could function to their full potential.

The taste test at the end of the show that day, where the studio audience decides their preferred dishes, could not have been easy. By creating such diverse dishes from exactly the same ingredients the chefs could really only appeal to the palates of those in the room. The judgement of which dishes were better was simply a matter of taste, voted by popular ballot. Fans of the show will have come to realize that the winner is rarely the chef with the greatest ability or imagination. Those who prefer to produce good slow-cooked food from the finest ingredients, and using the most skilful techniques, need not turn up for *Ready Steady Cook*. The chef who produces steak and chips will be voted the winner every time.

What has all of this to do with discipleship and evangelism in the contemporary church? Well, we are much like the chefs on *Ready Steady Cook*. We have a range of possible ingredients 'given' in the store cupboard – which we discussed in Chapter 1. These come from God's self-revelation: creation; fall; covenant; Jesus and the cross resurrection; new creation; and consummation. Then we have today's ingredients brought to us 'in the bag' – cultural ideas that vary with time and place, from generation to generation – the ingredients discussed in Chapter 2. Together, these different ingredients are the materials out of which, given our training and a little inspiration, we fashion our recipes and menus.

But then, when we start to cook, we realize that even more considerations come into the picture. Otherwise, the dishes we produce would all look exactly the same. And let's face it, they don't! How do we account for the differences between Christians who have basically the same things in the store cupboard, and in the bag, but come up with extraordinarily different recipes for evangelism? Why do some believe in crusade-style preaching, and others in friendship outreach? Why do some prefer to be confrontational, while others refuse to offer a challenge to belief at all? Didn't we train at the same chef college under the same Good News Gourmet?

A hundred years ago, two hymnwriters took the ingredients that were in their kitchens, and came up with two very different songs. They had the same basic ingredients, and the same variable ones. The presence of Jesus was very important to both of them. They were both influenced by an interest in social problems and the concern of God for humanity. There was also a lot of interest in the end times in the air.

William Merrill came up with a hymn called *Rise Up O Men of God*. The third verse reads

> Rise up O men of God
> The Kingdom tarries long
> Bring in the day of brotherhood
> And end the night of wrong.

The hymn is an invitation and inspiration to continue serving one another in love, and work to bring God's kingdom to earth.

Eliza Hewitt was writing at about the same time. She penned the hymn, *When We All Get to Heaven*. Her obvious optimism aside, she responded to the same challenges as Merrill by writing

Onward to the prize before us
Soon his beauty we'll behold
Soon the pearly gates will open
We shall tread the streets of gold.

She responded to the trials of life by thinking of the glory to come not on earth, but in the kingdom of heaven where there will be no suffering or pain.

If I were to do a quick taste test, which hymn would you choose? Whatever you decide, it may well reveal more about the ideas that are 'in the air' for us in the church today, than it does about which hymnwriter was the better chef. The seasonal ingredients have a greater effect on us than we can imagine sometimes. Survey your friends and find out whether they all choose the same one. If they do, you can learn a lot about the contemporary palate from a very simple exercise. There are probably aspects of each hymn that we would wish to affirm, and those we would wish to deny, or at least see stated another way. But there is a reason why two hymnwriters, handed the same ingredients, could come up with two very different dishes.

In addition to the 'givens' in the store cupboard of our kitchens, we also have a number of factors that give our recipes flavour and leaven. The good news gourmet brings to the kitchen the living and active word of God. We bring our own belief, that is our faith as a personal commitment to Jesus Christ, we bring our confession that he is Lord of our lives, and we bring our personal and community experience of the world. We bring our tradition, and all the power of imagination fired by the Holy Spirit. Let's consider some of these extra ingredients briefly, in turn.

God's living and active word

We considered in Chapter 1 how the Bible and our understanding of God form the stock ingredients of our recipes for discipleship and evangelism. But God's word is not locked in an ancient book, as though he is bound within its pages. The Bible is our sufficient and reliable account of God's revelation, and its meaning. That is not to say that because God lives in the Bible he lives there alone. By his Holy Spirit, God is alive in our world today, in our lives, in our communities. He comes to us 'new every morning'. Not so we won't recognize him when he turns up, but as the Creator and re-Creator, he is able to meet us in each situation of our lives, and bring his truth to bear upon it. This is his creative initiative and not our invention. We need to allow him room to speak, to challenge, to correct our actions and activities as churches now.

We can't be let off the hook of knowing what the Bible teaches, and how it works out in the world today. There are no shortcuts. If we hope to discern

IF WE HOPE TO DISCERN WHAT GOD'S LIVING AND ACTIVE WORD IS SAYING TO US TODAY, WE NEED TO STUDY THE BIBLE AND BE FAMILIAR WITH WHAT IS COMMUNICATED THERE.

what God's living and active word is saying to us today, we need to study the Bible and be familiar with what is communicated there. As we study the pages of scripture, with our present situation in mind, we'll be surprised how clearly its words will speak, and its message will challenge and comfort. We really will find guidance for life, today. We really can expect to hear God speak to us afresh through its words. It takes discipline and consistency to get the most out of the Bible. It's not just about being clever, but about approaching the word with humility and earnestness.

We're not in this task alone. Remember the letter in Revelation to the church in Pergamum? 'I know where you are living,' the Lord says. 'I know your situation. I know your temptations, your trials, your frustrations. I know how hard you try, and how miserable you feel when you fail. I know your confusion, and your insecurity.' How does he know all this? Because he is here with us. If God is here with us, then we need to be prepared to be surprised by the Holy Spirit now and then. It's his leaven that will help our dough to rise. We're not on our own. It's his work that he's doing through us. We need only make ourselves available. It may be hard graft sometimes, but what a relief to know that bringing in the kingdom is something he's capable of handling. When the things we do are Spirit-initiated and Spirit-directed, we are free from the pressure of thinking it's all up to us. And we can enjoy cooking, rather than merely endure the heat of hell's kitchen!

Our experience of the world

We all come to the Bible with the memory and formative quality of our own life experience. We are embodied, historical creatures, and it can't be any other way. When we encounter a particular biblical truth, it rings true because it connects somehow with our experience of the world. When I read that Jesus liberates, I think of my sin, and my personhood as a woman. For someone in central America, it may connect with their desire for freedom from poverty and political oppression. We make the same statement, and mean different things by it, because our experience is so different. But ultimately, we must appeal to those basic ingredients and use the Bible as our touchstone. It may be incorrect for me to say that Jesus liberates me as a woman. I need to understand the Bible in its own setting in order to get as clear a picture of Jesus as possible. And then I apply my understanding to my experience. It goes both ways, and involves a continual dialogue. We come to the Bible in light of our experience, and ask the Bible to correct our perceptions and speak back to our experience. We may well bring our questions to the text, but we also have to allow the text to ask questions of us. This is how we ensure that our discipleship is directed, and not simply accidental. This gives our discipleship direction, meaning, and formation. Otherwise, we're left with a string of fateful coincidences to define our lives in Christ.

It's not only our personal experience that conditions our approach to evangelism and discipleship. The experience of our community is also part of the picture. Communities help us identify areas of our personal experience that need to be challenged, but sometimes, communities can give false credibility to ideas that are flawed. A bad idea can live a lot longer in a community than is likely when it is the idea only of a single individual. Similarly, a good idea can be preserved in a community even when individuals have forgotten or rejected it. Our community embodies our tradition, regardless of whether that tradition is new or old. And new or old, tradition can be a rudder that steers our life together, or an anchor that weighs us down.

I was once part of a church that worshipped in an enormous building. It was big enough to seat 1100 people, and we rarely got more than 11 for services. When I began to enquire about possible alternatives for how we could use the buildings, I was quickly put in my place. I was made to realize that the opportunity for change had been rejected years before. A large supermarket chain offered a significant amount of money to the church, on top of constructing a brand new building in the middle of an expanding housing estate. It sounded like a God-given opportunity to me, but not everyone agreed. The church

members had a huge row. The people who wanted to go
ahead with the project ended up leaving the church, while
the people who didn't want any change made sure to get
the building listed. When some were accused of hindering
the future ministry of the church, they were recorded in
church minutes as offering a harsh reply. Some said that
their fathers had laid stones for that church building, and
they had been baptized, married, and had their children
dedicated there. As long as the church doors were open at
their funeral, they didn't much care what happened to it
after that! I was no longer surprised by the dire situation
in which they found themselves years later. For them,
tradition was an anchor that weighed them down and
prevented them from having their sails filled with the
wind of the Spirit.

On the other hand, I know of another church in a
different location that had a similar offer at about the
same time. They realized that their building was originally
built because a leader many years ago dared to dream a
big dream. The way that they could be faithful to that
tradition was to learn to dream big dreams as well. They
negotiated with savvy, and a large multinational company
helped them develop their premises in a way that prepared
them for the opportunities for ministry in a changing
community. For them, tradition was a rudder that helped
them steer through treacherous waters.

Tradition, then, can be good or bad. It's bad when we
think that being faithful to it entails repeating the same
actions and patterns over and over again. It's good when
we think of tradition as a testing-place and a guide.
Tradition allows us to grab hold of those things that have
been tested over time and found to be good, strong, and
lasting. It encourages us to follow the patterns of those in
the past who ventured for Christ, dared to have a dream,
and make the dream happen. Tradition bears witness to

the corporate experience of the church, and helps us to make wise decisions in light of the successes and mistakes of the past.

The way we *think*

When we read scripture, meet with God, and relate his truth to the world of our experience, we do it in partnership with our grey matter. I used to tell the kids in my youth group not to leave their brains at the door when they went to the cinema, or when they went to church. We don't have to be cultural victims, simply following along the easiest road, the path of least resistance, in understanding what the Christian faith is all about in the world today. Being created by God implies that we have the ability to think. He invites us to 'Come let us reason together.'

The way we think involves our thought processes, and draws on all the resources of reason and logic that God has given to us. This is not to say that we can reason our way to God, or that if we think hard enough, we'll fathom God with our brains. But God gave us brains to grasp his revelation, to understand what it means, and to apply it to the world as we encounter it. Although our reason may not prove God's existence, it can help us to test which claims about God are true, and which ones do not make sense. Reason can help us to explore which aspects of our culture need correction, and which ones can be rightly affirmed. Reason helps us to make sense of the competing claims around us.

This means that it's not sufficient for us to simply say what a particular Bible passage means for us at the moment. It's not enough to say this is how the world is, so this is how it's meant to be. We need to really understand scripture, how it holds together with other aspects of revelation, how it coheres when we apply it to the world in which we live. We can bring our tough questions and search for answers as we seek deeper understanding of who we are as Christians in the world, and what God intends for us to do here.

I knew a woman who was a new Christian who lived on a rough estate, and had lots of edges that God was working on – much like all of us! I was surprised one day to hear her say that she must have lost her job because God meant for her to lose her job. When I pursued this with her, it turned out that she firmly believed that everything that happened in the world happened because it was how God wanted it. When she started dating a guy half her age, it was because God meant for them to be together. When she fell pregnant with his child, it was because God intended for them to have a child. It never occurred to her that her own will and reason could affect these events in any way. She needed a good dose of reason, but she was having none of it. Being reasonable would mean being responsible, and she found that a step too much to take.

When we relate our faith to the world, we can draw on evidence that we see around us that supports our belief in the existence of God. We can reason about how that physical evidence fits together with biblical evidence, and the evidence that comes through our experience. We can develop our understanding of how these things fit together, and why they sometimes are contradictory.

Have you ever been in a book club or film club? I've found them to be invigorating but frustrating experiences. On too many occasions after reading a provocative book, or seeing a stimulating film, the discussion has resorted to a retelling of which bits we liked and which we didn't like. It's sometimes been harder than pulling teeth to get people to really *think* about what they read, or what they saw. How does it challenge your beliefs? How does it grow your faith? What does it say about our culture as a whole? What does it say about us? I once went out on a limb, passionately describing how *The Lord of the Rings* resonates so deeply with my experience of the Christian community. I regaled about life's faith journey, and how the popularity of the films showed a longing in our culture for trust in our relationships, and integrity in our tasks. I finished my heartfelt analysis, and asked if anyone else would like to say anything. 'Well I thought Frodo had awfully big feet,' one woman offered.

We've really got to seek more than an emotional, gut reaction to our culture if we ever hope to engage with it as Christian disciples with integrity. We've got to feel, and engage our emotions. That's important. But we've also got to *think* if we're going to incorporate our feelings into understanding. A chef needs to understand how various ingredients will respond when they are added to the mix of the recipe. In the same way, we need a reasonable appreciation of what will happen when we blend particular ingredients, and what the possible outcome might be. If you mix baking soda and vinegar, you'll get lots of fizz. If you add yeast to water that's too hot, you'll kill it. Some things go well together and some things do not.

Reason tells us that we don't give hour-long sermons to teenagers whose attention span is five minutes on a good day. Reason encourages us not to wear a suit when we're going to minister on the streets. Reason helps us make recipes that will actually connect with people, because we understand what they're about and what we're about. We use our reason to help us make the connections between revelation, past experience, and future possibilities. When we're going to prepare the feast, we dare not leave our brains at the kitchen door.

Our belief

Our belief is not just a list of doctrines where we tick off the appropriate boxes. Rather, our belief is very personal, it is part of who we are, and it represents our very real commitment to Christ. There are communal aspects of our belief and there are individual ones. In practice, almost all of our cooking begins with our own faith.

Our faith is our commitment to God, how we understand God, and what we believe about him. It is that thing that binds us to him when it seems like our brains aren't working, and neither is life. When our experience seems to shout, 'There is no God!' our faith leads us to believe. In the face of doubt, discouragement, and despair, faith persists.

Our belief is very simply our confession that regardless of what we experience, and how we struggle to apply the Bible to life, Jesus is lord. We own it individually when we make a public profession of faith, through baptism, or in sharing communion. It is a corporate concept, in the sense that it makes us part of the church universal, a member of the priesthood of believers from the first century till now. It binds us together with believers the world over, and grafts us into the body of Christ. Making our confession of Christ, we break bread and drink wine, and proclaim his death till he comes again.

OUR BELIEF IS VERY SIMPLY OUR CONFESSION THAT REGARDLESS OF WHAT WE EXPERIENCE, AND HOW WE STRUGGLE TO APPLY THE BIBLE TO LIFE, JESUS IS LORD.

This is more than a 'God said it, I believe it' simplistic view of life. It is the mark of the Spirit, that God claims his believers for himself, and nothing can prevail against them. Believers in Christ are assured of his indwelling Spirit that nurtures faith, and helps it to grow. Our belief, our commitment of faith, our confession of Christ, helps us to continue preparing the feast, even when the circumstances of life discourage us and tell us it's not worthwhile. Sometimes, despite what we see all around us, we believe. And this is the place where we can really start to cook.

Beyond the taste test

Like a gourmet, and not a fast-food chef who merely flips and fries, we need to serve up good honest simple food from the finest ingredients, appealing to the palates of the audience without compromising our technique. We need to have the skill, knowledge, and imagination of the gourmet, but be able to turn it out in fast-food time. We need to be able to serve up the good news in a form that can win the taste test without undermining the ingredients. And we need to recognize that sometimes, even the gourmet will lose the taste test. But there will always be discerning palates who are seeking the most unique and authentic flavours, and the chef who is able to bring out the best from quality ingredients.

How do we avoid simply giving in to a 'taste test' culture? How do we know when the recipes we've concocted are actually good ones? Is it possible to mix Bible and belief, reason and experience, tradition and imagination in such a way that we achieve a good balance of flavours and textures? And how will we know when we've got it right?

First of all, we need to remember that we'll never get it perfect. That should make us humble gourmets. But like all good gourmets, we can learn what gives a good balance of flavours and textures. This helps us to build confidence, even when we're cooking for an unfamiliar crowd. There are clues that will help us recognize when we've got too much of the special ingredients and not enough of the basics. There are flavours that complement and flavours that clash. And we can all get too comfortable making the same dish over and over, and forget about the gift of imagination. There's room for returning to old faithfuls when you're uncertain, but more often than not, a little adventure is worth the risk.

I had a teacher once who awarded extra marks for creativity. Even if the attempt failed miserably, he believed that it deserved reward, because of the risk it carried. That encouragement to take the risk of creativity made a mark on me that has stayed with me through years of ministry and teaching. Sometimes, it does fail. But most often, I've found it to be worth the risk. It's certainly never boring! And over time, I have grown confident in taking certain risks, and learned that others should not be touched. At the same time, I'm always ready for the possibility that my creative approach may not work, and I hope that gives me an appropriate humility, without killing my willingness to be vulnerable later on.

There's always a chance, too, that in any group there will be some who don't appreciate your creativity. They need to be dealt with sensitively, but they shouldn't necessarily set your agenda. I remember one series of missions we did through local churches. There was a man on our team who didn't like some of the more dramatic things we wanted to try. 'I'm not doing anything that I feel is silly,' he insisted. We didn't think it was silly, but we thought it was more important to have his participation than not, because he related to an entirely different segment of the community than the rest of us. In that case, it was better to drop some of the creativity. On another occasion, I was reading a conference paper that was creative and visual in its approach – not quite what you might expect from an academic paper. A number of colleagues enjoyed the approach, but one rose to his feet to declare pejoratively, 'Well, THAT was different.' In this case, I thought it was worth addressing his objection, but without apology, since he was in the extreme minority, and I felt it was still the best way to present some energetic ideas. But even a little criticism can take the wind out of your creative sails. Creativity involves risk, and it is not for the faint-hearted.

On still another occasion, I was responsible for an evangelistic campaign throughout a rural region in Canada. I thought it would be fun to develop it under a wild west theme, and recruited some local ministers to dress up as tough cowboys. We posed them for pictures and produced 'Wanted' posters and flyers. (Jesus wants them and he wants you was the idea.) We stuck their tough guy images in post offices and shops through the towns and villages. We developed some promotional skits based on the preacher from the east defeating mean but bumbling characters, and presented them in various services throughout our communities. Most people laughed – a lot! A few people complained. You know who they were, too. People who had been in church their whole lives, but for some reason, couldn't see the need for a creative approach to engaging those outside of the church. We decided to stay the course for a while, but in response to the criticism, tailed off the skits as time went on. Much to our surprise and delight, our comedy sketches had to be resurrected when we began the evangelistic meetings. We got word from some communities that a number of unchurched people would come, but only if the cowboy preachers were there! We had to do a lot of improvisation, but the meetings were a great success as a way for the churches to begin to engage with their wider communities.

If the point of the skits had been simply to laugh – we'd have moved into the realm of entertainment alone. But they all had a significant spiritual point, and using laughter and drama drew people in to connect with what was happening. There was a biblical message to each sketch, demonstrating that scripture doesn't have to be dry to be serious. Even *we* were surprised by the way God used our meagre attempts at creativity. Clearly we can be biblically based in our evangelism while still connecting to the unchurched community.

Balancing flavours and textures

The good news gourmet seeks to provide a healthy balance of nutrients, with wholesome flavours and interesting textures. When in doubt, all the other ingredients should be balanced in relation to scripture as the main ingredient. But even then sometimes we might disagree, and for that we need grace – handling a certain degree of diversity.

But this diversity is not absolute. There is certainly room for judgement to say that some things are simply not good recipes at all. There are some that contain too much of one ingredient, and no matter how long you bake the cake, it's not going to rise! Even some things that become very popular among Christians are not necessarily made from good recipes.

Remember the Prayer of Jabez phenomenon? The idea was that if you prayed a particular, and somewhat obscure, Old Testament prayer each day, you would see God do amazing things in your midst. It became a marketing sensation. There were Prayer of Jabez books, mugs, blankets, and mint wrappers. There were Prayer of Jabez books for nurses, pastors, teachers, police officers, cats, and budgies. Somebody, presumably, made a lot of money, and probably, somewhere, some people were blessed through it (though perhaps more because of God's grace than any power derived from chanting a mantra). But it was a relatively short-lived phenomenon, and few could say their discipleship grew leaps because of saying it every day. Why do you think it had the shelf-life of a hot cross bun? Well, let's look at how it balanced out some of the ingredients we consider essential to a good recipe.

First of all, it was based on Scripture. So far so good. But remember that we need to avoid cherry-picking verses, and consider the whole of the Bible. The many verses that speak of self-sacrifice, counting the cost of discipleship, and God's sovereignty over our affairs despite miserable appearances, should have sounded a warning bell to any who thought they'd found a magic formula to successful living. A cartoon I saw summed it up perfectly in a split image. The first half of the frame depicted a rich man with an enormous mansion, blossoming gardens, and frolicking animals. In the second half of the frame another man stood next to the rich man's fence. But his house, his fields, his clothes, everything was in ruin. The devastated man is reaching his hand over the fence and introducing himself said, 'Hello, you must be Jabez. I'm Job, your new neighbour.'

By praying the prayer, what kind of success were we looking for? Enhanced property portfolios, new business deals, health and prosperity? The expectations of many seemed out of step with other important elements of scripture, including the story of Job. Although Scripture was central to the phenomenon, it was restricted to just a few verses extracted from their context and favoured over other portions of Scripture that required equal or greater consideration. For example, Scripture has much more to say about justice for the poor and freedom for the oppressed than many other matters that regularly grab our attention.

Next in our recipe test, we need to ask how the Prayer of Jabez phenomenon resonated with our experience of the world. Was it an authentic representation of our needs and desires? Did it affirm or deny how we know life to be, based on our real experiences of life? Well, perhaps it reflected an acknowledgement that all aspects of our lives are out of our control and in need of God's touch. It reflected a desire among many to surrender aspects of our working lives to God. In this sense, it represented a real desire to see God at work in every corner of life, from work and family, to church and finances. At the same time, it affirmed our consumer culture by encouraging our desire for individual success. The anxiety we experience in our culture today in our striving for status, recognition, fame and wealth was hidden in the security of a prayer. Not sure if you're getting up, keeping up, moving up? Let God take care of it. Pray this prayer, and just in case your talents and efforts aren't enough, maybe God will take up the slack. Based on our contemporary experience of the world, we should not be surprised that the prayer was a marketing success. But we should be dismayed by it, when we consider the experience of the whole community of faith.

When we consider the tradition of the church, its experience in history, and its contemporary experience around the world, it seems that the prayer of Jabez is hard to pray. Prayers for enlarged territory and assured blessing? It is good to be humbly confident, but whenever the church has aspired to worldly power, it forgot its mission. With the crusade journeys in our family photo album, and the daily suffering of the church through persecution in many places in view, it seems that the Jabez prayer doesn't necessarily resonate with the experience of the whole community of faith. Success and blessing for many Christians means having a meal in their bellies and a roof over their heads.

Or it means simply living to see another day. Given this reality, the prayer phenomenon may have resonated with western experience of the world. But in light of the experience of the whole community of faith, it is found disconnected and wanting.

And what do our reason and imagination say? Reason tells us that there are no magic solutions to life, that God doesn't ask us to be successful, but faithful. However, our imagination allows us to dream. It encourages us to consider how God's kingdom might be enlarged, and grow through our lives. So the prayer is not necessarily reasonable, but it does connect with a reflective imagination. Considering its imbalance of several ingredients, we perhaps should have been more suspicious of it as a phenomenon that would have a lasting impact on the life of the church, with relevance for Christian discipleship and evangelism.

Engaging our culture in light of our faith, and vice-versa, requires a degree of coherence. There has to be balance of flavour and texture if we are going to engage culture in a way that assists our own growth as disciples, and informs our approaches to evangelism. Engaging culture has to entail much more than showing film clips in sermons, or reading a book together in your home group. In order for the engagement with culture to be a real engagement – much like a dance – then we need intentionally to reflect on our encounters with culture, and bring our biblical worldview to bear on what we watch and read and see. Similarly, if we are to allow the Bible to speak effectively to needs today – indeed to diagnose them – we need to remember that we are members of a culture ourselves. Unless we're

ENGAGING CULTURE HAS TO ENTAIL MUCH MORE THAN SHOWING FILM CLIPS IN SERMONS, OR READING A BOOK TOGETHER IN YOUR HOME GROUP.

going to seal ourselves off in caves (and some days I must admit I'm there with the old hermit monks!), we have to be able to bring our faith and the world into helpful and reflective conversation.

In their book *The Art of Theological Reflection*, O'Connell, Killen and de Beer examine how we bring things like God's word to overlap with our culture. For our purposes, we can think of them now as two large mixing bowls, one containing the stock ingredients, and one containing the day's special ingredients. Some people are content to live completely in the realm of one or the other. But unless we mix them together, our recipes are not going to work. If you took the potatoes and spinach and cheese and mixed them together in one bowl, and the milk and eggs in another, and cooked them separately, you certainly wouldn't have a Spanish omelette! Nevertheless, some people are afraid of what might happen when they mix the two, so they avoid it. Or, the mixing seems like such hard work that they can't be bothered. But it is worth the effort. And we can have fun.

We end up with a bad recipe when we refuse to do any mixing at all, or if we just dump the contents of one bowl into the other without stirring them properly. What happens when we end up with a bad recipe? How can we tell it's bad? The most obvious way is by the results. What does it look like, and how does it taste? Good recipes, on the other hand, see the mixing as critical to the final outcome of the dish. Look through your cookbook. For each recipe, there's the list of ingredients, and then the method. Some recipes require little method – we like those ones after work on a busy day. You just throw everything into the bowl, stir and cook. But there are other recipes that have a rather involved method. Some recipes are for the more skilled cook who is used to the intricacies of baking, and others have a straightforward method suitable for beginners. Whether a skilled chef or a beginner, there are basic skills that must be learned in order to stir the ingredients properly. Egg whites need to be folded in, and pastry needs to be worked well. The method of stirring is an exploration into possibilities of what God can do in us and through us when we're willing to take the risk of creativity. And the best gourmets learn to thrive on risk, because risk creates opportunities. Let's look at some of the possible outcomes when we don't get the mixing right, and we end up with a poor balance of flavours and textures.

SELF-CENTRED *v.* SELF-ASSURED

For those who prefer to work only with the stock ingredients, there is a danger that they can produce recipes that are so self-assured that they are virtually arrogant. There is no room for discussion with unchurched people, or with any aspect of culture. There is an assumption that the content of the gospel is narrowly defined, and its meaning self-evident to all. Any who disagree with a particular interpretation of Scripture and doctrine are outside of the fold, and mistaken.

On the other hand, there are some who prefer to work solely with the locally available produce. They face the danger of being self-centred. They are likely to interpret life, indeed Scripture, on the basis of their own experience of life. If it doesn't make sense to where they're at in life at the moment, they dismiss it as unhelpful and irrelevant. They are happy to throw away treasured beliefs of others because they don't happen to see their usefulness. Those who differ with them are regarded as old, traditional, narrow, and unloving.

Mixing these two together takes skill and practice. But the place of imagination and exploration will yield a recipe that is God-centred and God-assured. We'll be reminded that our perspectives are limited, and so we need to touch in with God's story. At the same time, we'll recognize that our story is of interest to God; that even though we don't know what's going on sometimes, God's presence is assured. He is the author of both his story and ours. We needn't panic about getting it perfect, because he's there, in the mixing.

HOBBYHORSES *v.* BIBLICAL NEGLECT

Those who prefer to work with the standard ingredients also face the likelihood of riding hobbyhorses in their discipleship and evangelism. Because they are not encountering any challenge from outside of their biblical perspective, they are likely to develop favourite methods, verses, and sermons for use in their approach to others. Rather than listen, they will ride their hobbyhorses till the cows come home. They may still be using old methods long after they've passed their sell-by date. And they'll not be able to understand why they should 'change' because they will not be in touch with what is actually going on in culture at any given time.

Then there's those 'spring-green' types who figure the Bible's not worth talking about in evangelism and discipleship because, let's face it, we only make it say what we want to anyway. More than that, God doesn't love us more when we're reading it, focusing on it. We're just as likely – more likely – to encounter God in the pub, at the club, or having a smoke with friends, as we are to meet him in the pages of an ancient book. Such people are motivated by a connection to culture that causes them to neglect the Bible altogether.

But begin to mix the two together. Our favourite passages are challenged by contemporary questions. Contemporary lifestyles are challenged by the questions

Scripture asks us. When we begin to mix them together, we will discover a biblical breadth and depth that increases our understanding and motivates our mission. As a result we'll see and understand our culture better, and be able to read it and respond more effectively. Real communication will result, rather than all talking, no listening. I'm told by the wife of my former New Testament teacher that he doesn't hear as well as he used to. When she shouted up the stairs to ask if he posted the mail, he responded, 'No, I haven't spoken to Mary for some time.' Often our communication between church and culture is a lot like that. Somebody saying one thing, and somebody else hearing another. We end up talking at cross-purposes instead of talking about the cross with purpose.

SECTARIAN *v.* INDISCRIMINATE

Those who use only store-cupboard ingredients find it very easy to draw lines and dare other Christians to cross so that they can rejoice to remove the heretic from our midst. They are certainly not the only ones who do this, but they are more prone to do it, because of their position of self-assurance about what is true. It can become a divisive stance, that looks to draw boundaries around cloisters of Christians who are 'orthodox' or 'acceptable'. Such lines may be drawn around specific beliefs, attitudes, or religious associations. It appears judgemental and exclusive.

Conversely, those who deal only with the ingredients of the day seem indiscriminate in their embrace. There is no-one who does not belong in the fold. Find somebody who thinks they are outside of the boundaries of the community and we need only redraw the boundary to take him in. But this position fails to take account of the fact that the guy standing outside may, in fact, *not* belong, and more than that, he may not *wish* to belong. Why draw a line around somebody that means nothing? You risk losing your own identity, and forcing one on him. At the same time, you do nobody any justice in your evangelism if you are not clear why you are interested in people in the first place. There are some who believe we ought not *ever* offer a word of challenge, correction, or exhortation to belief in the contemporary era. This does people a great disservice. We rob them of their dignity as God's creatures by refusing to give them an opportunity to respond to his invitation to belief and discipleship. And it's hard for us to grow as Christians without working out our discipleship intentionally within the community of faith.

Without organizing our community around some pretty convincing content that makes our community distinct, it's not long before we don't remember who we are or why we're supposed to love God and the world. Picture it – soon we won't even know who we are, or why we're supposed to love. Since it won't be clear what it is that we share in common, then we cease to be a community. We dissolve as the body of Christ. Our community is a body, and a body has form. And we can learn to speak body language.

Miroslav Volf in his book *Exclusion and Embrace* talks about how we need to express the body language of open arms, and embracing. In Volf's embracing, we make ourselves vulnerable, and see others with the kind of respect that says 'I welcome you as a human being, a fellow creature of God.' Certainly we need to practise this kind of body language, and speak it to those who are lonely, isolated, and marginalized.

But more than this, the Scriptures make it clear that new creations in Christ form the new covenant, and so it's not just anybody that is part of Christ's body, though everybody is welcome. People can't belong to the body regardless of what they believe or what attitude they might have to Christ. Embracing others means that our churches may well have woolly edges, but if we get a woolly centre, we may soak up too much liquid from our soggy culture and dissolve. We should be known for being a welcoming, embracing and loving community. But we are also required to be a discerning, searching, growing community under Christ.

INFLEXIBLE *v.* COMPROMISING

Using only our standard ingredients makes us inevitably inflexible. Once you've got hold of the truth, why let go? Yet we need to acknowledge that we don't possess the truth so much as the truth possesses us. For many, change represents compromise, and people who are inflexible fear compromise. This stands in stark contrast to a culture around us that is in constant flux and flow. Those who seem inflexible know that they have something good, and don't want to lose it. But at the same time, they risk living as a relic to the past rather than a compass to the future. Sometimes, they may confuse what is changeable with what is unchanging. In other words, they may not recognize the distinction between form and function.

For example, worship is a function of the church. It's central to our essence, of what it means to be Christian. But we can worship in a form that uses a pipe organ, or a form that uses street percussion. The gift doesn't change, though its

IN ONE DESERT LOCATION, THE NEW CONVERT CLIMBS INTO A COFFIN, AND A CHURCH MEMBER KNOCKS THREE TIMES, IN THE NAME OF THE FATHER, THE SON, AND THE HOLY SPIRIT. THE CONVERT THEN EMERGES JOYFULLY FROM THE COFFIN, TO JOIN THE CELEBRATION OF WORSHIP.

package might. When we recognize this, it's much easier for us to adjust to various forms of worship, regardless of whether they suit our particular taste. In some parts of the world where water is scarce, Baptists don't use water. Shocking, I know! In one desert location, the new convert climbs into a coffin, and a church member knocks three times, in the name of the father, the son, and the holy spirit. The convert then emerges joyfully from the coffin, to join the celebration of worship. As a believer in Christ, and by God's grace, he identified with the death, burial, and resurrection of Christ, which is what baptism is all about. Same function, different form.

But there are those who deal too much with all that is changeable, and they become too flexible. They might well say, baptism isn't meant for those parts of the world that haven't any water, so we'll do away with it altogether. Or, they will forget what the function of worship is, and turn the service into entertainment instead. For them, compromise is the order of the day. There is nothing in their view that isn't up for grabs, and demands reinterpretation. For them, form becomes the preoccupation over function, and they exhaust themselves trying to keep up with the next new cultural fad in their Christian lives. Their cues are coming first from culture, and they never join up properly with Scripture.

What we need more than ever as Christians is integrity. This should be our aim as we begin to mix the ingredients together. According to the theologian Alan Sell, integrity refers to *honesty* and *wholeness*. We are honest about our commitment to Christ, and the demands he makes on our lives. We are honest about the limits to our knowledge and understanding, and we don't pretend to tell more than we know. We hold together the whole of biblical doctrine, with the reality of experience of life today. We see ourselves as disciples, and our role of evangelism, in light of the whole life of the church, through history, and around the world. We are honest about how much and how little we know, and we want to reflect the totality of Christ in our lives, and the work he has done, in as much as we are able. We are not perfect in our mixing, but we seek to be faithful in our preparation of the feast, that what we have to share might be both an authentic representation of our traditions, and a fresh new taste to those who have never tasted real food before.

4

Recipes Old and New

4

Recipes Old and New

Choosing recipes: Christ and culture

Back in the 1950s, an American scholar named H. Richard Niebuhr published a book that became a classic. It was called *Christ and Culture*, and it was the first time anyone had tried to describe the various attitudes of the church towards culture throughout history, and group them together in types. In recent days, his ideas have come under a lot of criticism, because many people don't believe that the relationship between faith and culture is as simple as he made it out to be. Our explorations in this book so far would bear out some of that criticism. Nevertheless, his outline is a helpful starting-place when we're trying to assess our own attitude towards the culture in which we live. A brief glance at his 'recipes' will help us evaluate our own. Although he outlined six basic types, they can really be summed up in three basic attitudes.

CHRIST AGAINST CULTURE

This is the idea that our faith and our culture are diametrically opposed to one another. It highlights Scriptures that call us to be separate from the world, and is reflective of a doctrine of God that emphasizes his distinctness from his creation. It can be manifested in extreme forms, for example by those who retreat to live a monastic life away from public contact, or by entire families in community such as the Amish people in the United States. They separate themselves from what they consider 'worldly' pleasures and inventions, including anything from zippers on clothes to tractors, cars, and radios.

The Christ against culture theme does not always appear in such extreme forms, however. Many of us may encounter a philosophical idea, a social trend, or a political policy that we oppose on the basis of our faith. Very few elected representatives in Britain's parliament oppose our abortion laws, but many Christians do. Philosophies that deny the possibility of relationship with God, or a general decline in the standard of television programmes, may represent things that we believe are contrary to a Christ-centred life.

There are elements of just about any culture at any point in history that would seem to stand in opposition to Christian discipleship. We could find many things to oppose and protest against. And in fact, we often do. Evangelicals are popularly known for being anti-everything – anti-sex, anti-gay, anti-everything-that's-fun-and-can't-be-good-for-you. We have earned a reputation for being agitating alligators, who fix our jaws on something we fancy, and won't let go. Sometimes our reputation as alligators is undeserved. For one thing, we actually are in favour of just as many things in our culture as we oppose. The media seem to enjoy focusing on the things that we're largely against. It's easiest for evangelical leaders to get media spots when the reporters are looking for someone to criticize a particular development in culture or politics. But this creates an unbalanced picture of evangelical life.

Another reason our reputation for being agitating alligators is undeserved is because evangelicals seem increasingly insecure about social protest. We're embarrassed by values that run so unfashionably against the grain of culture. So we often remain silent when we have an obligation to stand up. When a BBC executive spoke at the graduation of the London School of Theology in 2003, he noted the embarrassment we often feel as Christians over the cultural joke that was made of Mary Whitehouse. She was irresistible to many as a target for humour because of her protests against television content. Our speaker pointed out the sad fact that we often join in the joke, and fail to realize that there are few people today willing to take the risk of unpopularity to stand against those things that starkly contradict our faith. A rude word here, some bare flesh there. Who cares? Suddenly its everywhere, even in Christian community. So much for discipleship that costs. So much for values, particularly the value of being different.

On the other hand, there are some places where the growl of the alligator *is* being heard. Christians are recapturing a sense of protest based on our social ethical values. Evangelicals were key to the launch and success of the Jubilee 2000 campaign. Many have been present in anti-war demonstrations and in fair trade campaigns in recent days. It is a movement that appears to be growing, and offers great potential for a positive cultural impact, even as we grow in Christ through our actions. It's a good opportunity to state positively some of the things we do stand *for* as Christians rather than simply being known as being *against* everything.

It's appropriate, then, to engage in protest for and against some aspects of our culture. Sometimes, we should be happy to have an alligator image! In other situations, the alligator image may be undeserved, but we have it nonetheless. How do we make it work for us? And how do we retain discernment about what's going on in our culture without becoming constantly antagonistic? There must be things in culture that we can affirm. It's important for us to find the balance when sharing the feast.

CHRIST OF CULTURE

Christians are no different from anybody else. We're just normal people. We meet Christ at work in the world, and get on board with what he's doing. God could be at work in any person, any group or organization. It's not being distinctly Christian that's important, but connecting with God's positive energy in the world.

This is the Christ of culture. This is the world of the 'cultural chameleon'.

Another way that faith encounters culture is from the inside of culture itself. The idea here is that God as Creator is the sustainer of all that is. He is present in the whole of his handiwork, and the distinction between Creator and creation is blurred. In the romanticist notion of encountering God in nature, there is no divide between what is natural and what is spiritual. However, for followers of any religion, there is usually a certain separation between things set apart for God, or for worship (sacred), and things that have no special religious significance (profane). Those who advocate a 'Christ of culture' view, seek God immanent in the world, rather than transcendent over it.

In contemporary times, this view does not distinguish between the creativity of humans and the creativity of God. Culture is not seen so much as a human creation as the almost accidental human environment in which we live. Believing that there's nowhere that God's Spirit is not present, people look for God not only in nature, but in art, film, and literature. You are just as likely to encounter

God in the cinema or at the Tate Modern as in a worship service. Where we used to view cultural manifestations with reflective suspicion, we now believe that it's not what enters human beings that corrupt them, but what comes out of them. There's nothing in our culture that's 'evil' in itself. It all depends on how it's used. Look for God in the strangest places, and you're likely to find him there.

I'm sure you know people who try to convince you that they can worship god just as well on a mountain-top as in church. Usually, they use this claim as an excuse not to go to church at all. My theological mentor has pointed out that despite flying over many

I'M SURE YOU KNOW PEOPLE WHO TRY TO CONVINCE YOU THAT THEY CAN WORSHIP GOD JUST AS WELL ON A MOUNTAIN-TOP AS IN CHURCH. USUALLY, THEY USE THIS CLAIM AS AN EXCUSE NOT TO GO TO CHURCH AT ALL. MY THEOLOGICAL MENTOR HAS POINTED OUT THAT DESPITE FLYING OVER MANY MOUNTAINS IN TRIPS ALL OVER THE WORLD, HE HAS YET TO WITNESS A SINGLE CHRISTIAN WORSHIPPING ON A MOUNTAIN-TOP.

mountains in trips all over the world, he has yet to witness a single christian worshipping on a mountain-top. When I asked him what he thought about those who insist they go to the cinema looking for an experience of God, he replied that they were just like the mountain-top worshippers – only with popcorn! Of course we can meet God in many places, but growing in discipleship should not entail a simple seeking-after-experience.

CHRIST TRANSFORMING CULTURE

Let your light shine. Get involved. Share Jesus at work. Let him make his mark in politics. This is our Father's world

– there's nowhere that he doesn't belong, and that Christ
can't make his mark. We can influence our world for good
as Christians so long as we're not afraid to get out there, get
involved, and sometimes get our hands dirty.

Christ transforming culture reflects the idea that culture
as a human creation can be directed and moulded.
This is the position that Niebuhr advocated, without
actually coming out and saying so. He believed that
God is everywhere but not everything is surrendered to
God's rule. We can use our influence in society to make
the instruments of government, Hollywood, and the
shopping cathedrals reflect Christian values. The idea
is to get in there and transform the things around us, by
living out our God-given gifts and calling in the culture in
which we live. Such a view is a helpful one for Christian
discipleship, as it acknowledges our distinction from the
world, while providing us with a task for engaging our
culture.

Despite its helpfulness, the idea of Christ transforming
culture through his church may lead us too easily to seek
power in our society. If we hope to transform culture, this
implies a certain degree of influence and participation in
the organs of social power. Many Christians are hesitant to
align the church with any instrument of power that could
corrupt our gospel motives. It is easy, as soon as you taste
power, to desire more power, and then to enjoy it for its
own sake. This view also encounters difficulty in that it
assumes that the goal of a Christian society is desirable.
For many Christians, however, we only understand our
identity when we are on the margins of society, and not
consciously seeking to be the dominant voice.

We can modify the idea of Christ (or faith) transforming
culture and present it in a more nuanced form. Seeing our
faith as being *in dialogue with culture* allows us to have a

distinctive view that is possibly transformative without being equated with the power structures that may too easily compromise our position as servants.

Being in dialogue with culture makes us interactive digital disciples. This approach is not so clearly defined, but it offers the possibility that sometimes we may need to stand against an aspect of our culture, and sometimes we may see Christ at work in the culture. Christ transforming culture is an ideal worth working towards, but there are contexts sometimes where it is a practical impossibility. The notion of dialogue helps us to recognize that our culture conditions our faith, and the traditional ingredients of our faith condition our culture.

Recognizing this dynamic interaction is one of the things that makes Christian faith so exciting today, even though it's not as easy to 'go to church' as it once was, when everybody did, regardless of what they believed. It was the culturally accepted thing. Now it's not. And can you blame people? We find all kinds of reasons to excuse the decline in regular church attendance in British society. Just as many people still attend at holidays, they still write 'Christian' in the faith box on their census forms, they look to the church for some kind of moral guidance. It's just that they don't come on Sundays any more. Those who are committed Christians use all sorts of excuses as to why they don't go, and many studies have been done plotting the graphs of leaders who have come in the front door running, and kept going down the aisle, across the platform and out the back door. There are as many reasons as people why this is so, as I think Alan Jamieson demonstrated in *A Churchless Faith*, his study of charismatic leaders in New Zealand who no longer go to church. But one of the main reasons I think we need to consider is that people have a choice today, where they didn't before when church attendance was the cultural norm. Duty is a bad word for us today.

Obligation sends us running. There are so few left doing their duty and fulfilling obligations that they get worn out, and sometimes they break.

Face it. We've all been there in one way or another. I've been a regular church attendee for most of my responsible life. The one exception was during my first year in ministry training. See the irony? Get the paradox? I was so busy studying theology, and reading the Bible and training to be a minister, that I couldn't be bothered to get up on Sunday morning and support one. But over time, I discovered a strong sense of duty. It's the kind of duty that pushes me out from under a warm and cosy duvet on a cold, dark, wet November morning to be part of a little group of people who gather once a week to meet with God *together*. Call it misplaced if you will. It may even be a dysfunctional reflection of a childlike desire to please.

BUT IS THERE ANYTHING WRONG WITH A CHILD SEEKING THE APPROVAL OF HER FATHER, EVEN THOUGH SHE KNOWS HE'LL LOVE HER JUST AS MUCH IF SHE'S LYING IN BED WITH THE PAPER ON SUNDAY MORNING AS IF SHE'S IN A DRAFTY BUILDING SINGING HYMNS? OF COURSE HE'LL LOVE HER JUST AS MUCH. AND SHE KNOWS THAT. BUT SHE RISKS FORGETTING HOW MUCH SHE LOVES HIM.

But is there anything wrong with a child seeking the approval of her father, even though she knows he'll love her just as much if she's lying in bed with the paper on Sunday morning as if she's in a drafty building singing hymns? Of course he'll love her just as much. And she knows that. But she risks forgetting how much she loves him. More than that, she risks becoming so individualistic that she focuses on her need to relax and be refreshed ahead of the need of others to be encouraged by the gifts she brings to worship. She forgets that part of discipleship is being together in the body of Christ. She begins to forget how she is encouraged when Mr Thornton tells her how good it is to see her smiling face, and how it lifts her heart to hear Sam's giggle when she tells him her latest silly joke. A small group of friends meeting in a pub can constitute something of what it means to belong to the body of Christ. But meeting together with people you would never normally choose to gather around you, representing all the diversity of the people of God, and bringing your praise, thanksgiving, and requests to him in unity, even after the squabbles and feuds ... well, I think that *really* makes God smile. And I don't mind that sometimes it takes a sense of duty to make me join in when I'd rather be doing just about anything else. That's worth getting out of bed for. And that's worth fighting for.

So this is something where it would seem that culture needs a kick in the ribs from the church. On the other hand, there are times when culture kicks the church. We should not be looking to have our every need fulfilled through our teaching, fellowship, and worship meetings. But if *none* of our needs are *ever* being touched, it's pretty difficult to grow in Christ. If you can't see the connection between the biblical text and your life, for example, you won't have any idea of how your life might be, could be, should be, different. If it's all just wrapped up in a Sunday package and doesn't infect the whole of your life and your relationships with family, and your behaviour at work, then it's pointless. A big part of what it means to 'be church' is to be equipped to live a distinctly Christian life in every context. And if church life isn't helping you to do that, demand better. Push beyond the fashionable criticism of 'the church'. It's not enough simply to moan about 'the church' like so many do. Those who are in Christ are part of the church. We are the very thing we criticize. So ask for help when you need it to make the relevant connection with your life. Take responsibility for your discipleship. And don't be afraid to ask questions. You'll usually find that five other people in the room were wondering the same thing.

Engaging our faith and culture in dialogue is a necessary conversation. And it's continuous. It has to be if we hope to make Christ contagious in a changing culture. How does our faith combine with our culture when we mix the two together? What recipes do we come up with when we see our faith in dialogue with various aspects of our contemporary culture?

We have, in our churches today, people who reflect various cultures and generations. It's impossible to talk about culture, even western middle-class culture, in any monolithic sense. It is a dynamic reality that resists strict categorization, as we have seen. Nevertheless, I think we can identify three general 'types' of people who represent different responses to the dialogue between faith and culture. The first group of people are the Frontier Scouts, the second are the Market Stall Vendors, and the third are the High Speed Networkers.

Frontier Scouts

Saddle up your horses! We're riding out across the frontier. It is a vast, open plain of opportunity and untold adventure. Like the great American cultural myth of the frontier, this wild west is one to be experienced, encountered, opened up, and conquered in the name of freedom. As we meet others in this place, we find them to be very different from ourselves. We find these chance encounters exciting, but threatening. Anyone who is different represents values that contradict the things that we hold dear. Some people may have to pay the price of preserving the kind of freedom that allows us to realize our values and ideals in our lives. The price is not too much to pay.

Frontier Scouts see the world as a hostile land to be conquered in the name of Christ. They scan the horizon, gather information and plot against the enemy. They see the world more in black and white than shades of grey. Truth is reasonably obvious to anyone with eyes to see. The conquered frontier represents harmony and prosperity for those who make the opportunities work to their advantage. Progress for the scout is seen as inevitable, and positive. Once you stake your claim, and build your homestead, you can build a decent life for yourself and your loved ones. You are self-determined in the sense that you simply want to live your life the way that you want to live, but you're happy to associate with others in community – even sacrifice for them – in order to achieve common purposes, and realize shared values and goals that will in turn increase the happiness of the individuals who comprise the community. The scout does not ask, 'Who am I?' Instead, the scout simply wants to know how to cope with the challenges of conquering a frontier without getting shot by outlaws.

In the church, you'll recognize frontier scouts as those who prefer to keep worship and leadership structures as traditional as possible. 'If it ain't broke, don't fix it!' Their view of outreach will be to bring people into the church, drag them kicking and screaming if necessary, and convert them to Christian values and way of living before embracing them as part of the community. Their approach to evangelism will be through reasoned apologetics, and proclamation, particularly through crusade-style meetings. And when it comes to how they approach change in the church? Um, did you say change? What change?!

COOKING FOR THE FRONTIER SCOUT

The grub on the trail is basic, but the work is hard, so any sustenance is appreciated. Chuckwagon beans, pickled eggs, and whatever game can be killed before dark to put hair on your chest. Lay out the feast on long wooden tables with benches. No table cloths or candles required, except on special occasions. No need for fancy chefs here. Or fussy palates!

DISCIPLESHIP: WHAT THE FRONTIER SCOUT WANTS

Frontier scouts are not afraid of hard work, risk, and adventure. You'll find them most often, though certainly not exclusively, among the older generation in our churches. Unfortunately, they are often categorized as traditional and inflexible. This may be true when it comes to values and forms of worship, but when it comes to outreach they usually are willing to do whatever it takes in order to accomplish the mission. Part of the reason why they may seem inflexible is because they have a long-time attachment to the things that give them consistency in a constantly changing world.

Generally, frontier scouts want people to be like them in some important ways. They deal best with those who conform to what has been demonstrated to be valuable and lasting. Because they have seen so much change over a lifetime, they are not easily swayed by trends. This can be a strength in that they will not be found riding every bandwagon that comes into town. It can be a weakness in that they may not understand how and when things have actually changed in a major way in society.

They understand duty, hard work, and self-sacrifice. They will find comfort from the disciplines of Bible reading and prayer, and will grow through doing things for others. Through the call of duty, they will discover what their gifts are, and how they can bless others. They will not necessarily find it easy to receive ministry from others around them; because they are resourceful, they are also self-sufficient. Their sense of duty may mean that sometimes, other activities with which they are involved may come before faith commitments. They will be prone to put family ahead of church, which in the long run means that their children may not inherit their faith, since it is seen as 'optional'.

DISCIPLESHIP:
WHAT THE FRONTIER SCOUT NEEDS

Frontier scouts need reassurance in the face of change. They need lots of face-to-face communication, and will then be able to trust what is happening around them. They will require lots of information, and also some activities designed particularly for them. When we consider that the fastest-growing segment of the British population is the over-65s, we ought to be able to welcome them into our church communities, not expecting them to be shoehorned into contemporary forms without offering a connecting place for them with others. Their experience of life and their diverse abilities need to be respected, and the gifts of time and ability they offer appreciated for the significance they hold for the church.

One of the things that frontier scouts need most for discipleship is cross-generational relationships. Too often, they are seen as 'past it' by the majority of younger people, who may avoid them in favour of more trendy people of their own age. This is a very unfair dismissal of people who are a treasured element of the body of Christ. With many contemporary calls to 'rethink' church, there seems to be a complete lack of consultation with those who have 'done' and 'been' church for a very long time. They need to be drawn into new discussions, and will have many helpful insights. I recently heard some young leaders of my own denomination make a presentation on their desire to see young people reached for Christ. They showed what they felt were shocking pictures of young, pierced, and tattooed youth to the largely older audience, and asked the question, 'Would you feel comfortable with these youth sitting beside you?' Many times, I have seen older people want to build serious connections with younger people. They are not shocked by them, they are desperate to know them. But it is often the young adults who do not want to go anywhere near the older folks. Frontier scouts prefer conformity, but they've had enough life experiences not to expect it!

More than that, several of the older members at that meeting had to admit that the feelings about church expressed by the alienated younger people were feelings that they sometimes shared. This was something that the young leaders had not considered. They had evidently never asked an older person if they ever experienced feelings of alienation from the Christian community, and ambivalence about its discipline. They missed an opportunity to discover coping strategies and growth points. All of this relates to Paul's exhortation to the older people to encourage the younger people, and the younger people to learn from the older people. If young and old are not mingling together and building authentic relationships, neither group is able to develop this aspect of their own discipleship. Solid discipleship for the frontier scout sometimes means setting aside the latest ideas, and listening to the voice of wisdom. It means standing against cultural trends that fragment society into groups of age or fashion.

EVANGELISM:
FRONTIER SCOUT RECIPES

Although the scout has much to teach us about the traditional basics of discipleship, we may run into difficulty with evangelism. Because evangelism is by nature more changing, some may find it difficult to reshape their ideas into new packages. They may become frustrated when their efforts seem to yield little fruit.

The basic frontier attitude to evangelism is that the State and the parish have some significant degree of responsibility in maintaining an overall Christian ethos in society. They will be disturbed by declining standards and values in public life, and will insist that schools maintain the major responsibility for Christian education of young people. They will be surprised that children in a 'Christian' country have not the least idea of who Jesus is. Or, if they are not surprised, they will decry the lack of Christian input in schools and by the governing authorities. Although they will be concerned about the growth and decline of Christianity, they may never have taken personal responsibility for sharing Christ with those around them.

On the other hand, some frontier scouts have been passionate evangelists. They rely on large gatherings like evangelistic crusades and tent meetings for preaching the gospel to as many people as possible. They will work tirelessly to set up prayer triplets and load a bus of people to go to a Billy Graham crusade. They may even volunteer and train as a prayer counsellor. This is an extension of the frontier attitude that looks to conquer culture. Throw the truth at as many people as you can possibly target. As an old fundamentalist preacher once said, 'Load your rifle with the buckshot of the gospel, and open fire!' Anyone with a reasonable grasp of reality will see how valuable and true it is, and respond. These scouts will often ask their minister why there aren't as many invitations for public response to salvation as their used to be. And they may lament over how long it's been since the last crusade came to town.

Younger scouts may work hard to set up well-meaning tent meetings, inviting a famous preacher or healer to speak. These events may find some degree of success. For one thing, our culture is used to large gatherings for sporting events and concerts. They may find sufficient security to attend such a meeting when they would be too shy to ever enter a church. Moreover, there are frontier scouts of every age, and there will always be those who see the world in the same way as our Christian scouts. Frontier Scouts are the best people to reach Frontier Scouts.

IT COULD BE, HOWEVER, THAT THE DAYS OF MASS RESPONSE TO THE PREACHED WORD OF CHRIST MAY WELL BE BEHIND US — AT LEAST FOR THE TIME BEING. IF WE INSIST ON SPENDING TIME AND RESOURCES PLANNING EVENTS THAT WILL NOT CONNECT WITH THE CONTEMPORARY MINDSET, WE MAY BE WASTING OUR TIME.

However, this approach to evangelism is likely to continue to decline. When we consider the bigger cultural picture, scouts are no longer in the majority in our society. There may be room for large events that use multimedia displays, and Christian concert events, where entertainment takes down barriers to acceptance of the gospel. Even then we have to be careful about manipulating emotions through mass responses to a message that may not really be understood by those indicating a response. It could be, however, that the days of mass response to the preached word of Christ may well be behind us – at least for the time being. If we insist on spending time and resources planning events that will not connect with the contemporary mindset, we may be wasting our time. Because the scout relates best to traditional ingredients, he may well produce traditional evangelism. And it just won't satisfy the appetite of the audience.

Market Stall Vendors

Meet me at the market. Not just any market – an organic farmers' market. Here, there are no two things alike. People are seen to sit like vegetables in the bin, all gathered together but completely independent, and isolated from one another. Truth? What is truth? It is completely subjective and relative. Show me your truth and I'll show you mine. Globalization will simply lead to conflict, because we are so different from one another that we're bound to clash. Progress is a meaningless illusion. You've got to just get in there every day, make what you can and get out. You're very insecure, and prone to self-doubt. And because you are so independent, community feels like a prison. Being together means you've got to adapt to others, and that's too much to ask because it's impossible. Christianity, just like every other religion, is laid out on display. You want it? – you buy into it. You don't? – then forget it. Stand and shout out your price, your specials. Some will take it and some will leave it.

You'll recognize Market Stall Vendors in the church by the way they seek individual experience in worship. They have a consumer attitude to church, and will shop around for the right programmes to meet their needs or the needs of their family. If a particular church community isn't meeting their needs any more, they will simply move on. They put God on offer, but shy away from personal approaches that require self-investment. For many, that means they won't actually engage in overt evangelism, but they feel their lifestyle is an example that should bear witness to their faith. If others see how they live and want to know more, they'll ask. They favour decisive change in the church, a strong leadership, and they may show a tendency of in-growth or repeated patterns of activity and behaviour.

COOKING FOR THE MARKET STALL VENDOR

Prepare an all-you-can-eat buffet. Make sure there are as many types of food as possible. Lay out the feast so people can access it from nearly any angle. This is food to go – standing-room only is required. The dishes are appealingly presented, and available in bulk. Chefs may be run ragged trying to cater to every taste. Fussy palates welcome.

DISCIPLESHIP: WHAT THE MARKET STALL VENDOR WANTS

The Market Stall Vendor has grown up alongside the development of the consumer society. In a world where you don't have to make many compromises in order to get what you want, and in a culture where you make multiple choices every day through purchase, vendors are used to assessing quickly the price and value of everything. They're also accustomed to getting their own way, getting what they want, and going elsewhere if they are not satisfied. They are not necessarily brand-loyal, and will assemble various identities appropriate to the various tasks in their lives.

A vendor is looking for discipleship tools whose use and relevance to their lives are obvious. They will think nothing of spending large amounts of money to attend the right event, buy and read the right books, receive the ministry and counselling that suits them. The vendor wants a church with a range of programmes on offer, something to meet their felt needs, and the felt needs of the other members of their family. They are comfortable shopping around for a church, and will choose the one that best suits their situation at a given point of their lives. More than that, they will think nothing of changing churches as their circumstances change, or when they feel that church is no longer offering the things that they need for Christian growth. They will seek out self-help groups, and are reluctant to become involved in anything that demands more than a short-term commitment. They enjoy small groups which function as part of a larger group, and are keen on communication and larger loose affiliations so that they can keep on top of the latest Christian trends.

DISCIPLESHIP: THE MARKET STALL VENDOR NEEDS

Vendors actually need some things beyond their felt needs in order to grow in Christ. Where the scouts cook their discipleship and evangelism with too many traditional stock ingredients, vendors cook their discipleship with too much fresh produce. Despite their independent stance as a consumer over and against the community of Christ, vendors need to be challenged by authentic community. They need to become involved in the lives of a wide range of people who are different from themselves in order to grow beyond their own self-perceptions. This could happen through mixed study groups that help them see different sides of various biblical and practical issues, or through involvement in social ministries with people they would normally avoid.

Vendors also need a lot of support. They find it easy to complain when the community is not living up to their expectations, but when the entire community is made up of people who flit in and out at will, who are, on average, time-poor and cash-rich, there is no one left to form the core where the heart of ministry beats. They need real community, but real community is very difficult to build in their midst. Their needs are apparent when we consider the suburban neighbourhoods where so many of them live. During the day, they are ghost towns, with adults all at work, and children spending long hours at school. The result is that homes lack a hearth – a warm meeting-place at the centre, which provides consistency and security for household members. Many routine tasks are hired out, paying others to repair, clean, and cook, even if it's just a takeaway.

This same pattern is echoed in the church. We've all heard of the man who listened to a very worthwhile ministry pitched at a meeting. He got out his chequebook and said, 'I haven't another hour to give, but whatever it costs, I'm willing to cover it.' Everybody is too busy to put in time. We're sometimes willing to pay others to do the work. But who's left to be paid to do it, when we're all so busy? Turns out, that the best things in life really do cost something, but they don't come with a price. The consumer attitude of the vendor needs to be challenged if they are to grow in discipleship.

EVANGELISM: MARKET STALL VENDOR RECIPES

The Market Stall Vendor responds to consumer-style approaches, such as leafleting, advertising, and non-

threatening seeker events. Alpha is an example of a programme that has had a great impact on vendors, through
its professional marketing strategy, small group nature,
and participation without obligation.

But some approaches to evangelism favoured by
vendors are not so successful. We recently had a new event
at my home church. Some people decided they wanted
to leaflet the neighbourhood around the church, which
includes a residential area, a shopping mall, and a busy
commercial district. They gave out hundreds of flyers,
most of which ended up in the bins and on the pavements
of Watford. They were dismayed at the rejection of their
offer, and discouraged when only one new face turned
up at the event.

The folks from my church were well-meaning, but they
were functioning as vendors with a frontier mentality. They
were putting their wares on offer in the market stall, but
were surprised when consumers chose not to buy. In the
main, our consumer culture is not interested in spirituality
that isn't trendy, that can't be
bought, or experienced in a
spa weekend. Those who are
spiritually inclined are either
post-consumerist, or needing a
personal contact to nurture the
spark of God-interest in their
lives. It just won't do to set out
the fruit and veg and hope for
the best. Christianity doesn't
fare well in the marketplace.
Its followers are unpopular, its
brand is flagging, and the price
is high. It's a spirituality that
costs everything. Buying into it
means losing your life in order

> CHRISTIANITY
> DOESN'T FARE WELL
> IN THE MARKETPLACE.
> ITS FOLLOWERS ARE
> UNPOPULAR, ITS
> BRAND IS FLAGGING,
> AND THE PRICE
> IS HIGH. IT'S A
> SPIRITUALITY THAT
> COSTS EVERYTHING.
> BUYING INTO IT
> MEANS LOSING YOUR
> LIFE IN ORDER TO
> FIND IT.

to find it. Not willing to take the risk? There's another stall on the other side of the market with a much easier path to inner peace. Why buy here?

High-Speed Networkers

Picture now a world connected through hubs of shared activity and interest, with nodes on the web forming and dissolving around particular interests. It is not a tangible picture, but like droplets of dew on a spider web at dawn, it is ethereal, and almost transparent. Rather than relate face-to-face with the same people for life, individuals encounter one another in various forms. At work and at home, we find our identity is formed from our participation in a unique combination of nodes. We are one person with one set of gifts and interests when we share our book club; we are another person with a different set of gifts when we join the anti-war protest. New nodes are formed when we need them, for example when we wish to gather information on a specific topic and we join virtual chat rooms or support groups. Others dissolve when they are no longer useful or necessary, say, when we quit the gym because it's winter and we don't have the imminent pressure of beaches and swimsuits. Our world is ordered around our needs and interests, and we make new connections and dissolve old ones with great rapidity.

For networkers, truth is not found in a single thought, idea, concept, or even person. Rather, truth is represented by a certain coherence that holds the various strands of life together, and makes sense of all of them. Truth is the thing that makes life 'work'. But it is also a mysterious thing – it's not necessary for us to possess truth, even if the pursuit of truth is a worthwhile search. Networkers are happy to live with this ambiguity, and it doesn't cause them anxiety. Globalization – the world community – is an accepted reality. It is a multi-directional fact of life, where we exchange views with many other views, where we are influenced by diverse people, and they are influenced by us.

Progress for the networker is personal and spiritual, and may have some political or social aspects. Networkers generally accept themselves, and find it easy to accept and include others, even those who are very different from themselves. Community is a positive concept for them, because community brings security. Christianity for them is not a quest or a struggle, but a journey. Often, it is a journey that is ill-defined. Although the path is individual, the travelling is best done in good company.

Networkers prefer alternative styles of worship, with lots of experiential and interactive content. They prefer participation to observation, and are suspicious of strong or authoritative leadership. They like a church with woolly edges, where people belong to the community before they make any commitment to faith. Outreach and evangelism are personal, based on one-to-one contact, and friendship groups. It involves a shared journey into faith, discovering Christ, rather than a one-off prayer of commitment. Change is expected and continual, and networkers are happy with experimentation, expect to be surrounded by multimedia, and can be very creative in thought and practice.

COOKING FOR THE NETWORKERS

This is the contemporary café, with comfortable soft furnishings, special dishes prepared in small quantities, to be enjoyed by clusters of friends. Serve food which is trusted and reliable at the whim of the chef; bistro dishes with an international twist. Food is made to order with fresh ingredients. Creative chefs and experimental palates are welcome.

DISCIPLESHIP:
WHAT NETWORKERS WANT

Networkers value authentic community above all else, a place where people are real, and they can be themselves. They want a place where they can seek after God, and explore the dimensions of their own spirituality in a creative context. They are self-conscious about bringing culture into spiritual contemplation. They want a sense of mystery, participation in leadership, and spiritual direction, and reject boundaries of tradition or expectation.

Networkers feel that they grow as they share stories, write poetry, reflect on cinema, and experience worship in diverse ways. The individual disciplines of Bible reading and prayer are not as important as meeting with friends at the pub. Since God is immanent in his creation, they don't feel the need to retreat alone in order to develop in discipleship. The result is sometimes a vague familiarity with Scripture, and methods of prayer. Since they value freedom and conscience, they will not see mutual challenge and correction as part of discipleship. They will find opportunities for Christian growth through social involvement and protest, as a way of witnessing to the goodness of God in a world that seems to have forgotten him.

DISCIPLESHIP:
WHAT NETWORKERS NEED

Networkers need to be reminded of the basic ingredients from time to time. It is important to challenge them on the value of tradition so that they can help to make the best elements of tradition live with relevance in the present. Bringing them into community with older people and those who see the world differently from them will challenge them to stretch their horizons. They will need to be encouraged to develop creative approaches for connecting with the traditional ingredients of faith as their culture emerges.

The provision of creative forums where their participation is valued is important for networkers. They will offer sustained periods of service so long as these are rightly balanced with the rhythms of retreat and spiritual feeding. They need affirmation as individuals, even as they rely on the intimate connections of community. They may occasionally need to be nudged on their attitude towards Christian commitment, and the content of discipleship. Many networkers are already mission-focused. This has implications for their discipleship in that they are so concerned about embracing the stranger that they may forget the reason for the welcome. On the other hand, they are seeking resources for protest and action, and are increasingly comfortable being an alternative community in a consumer culture. They need encouragement to participate in local community initiatives, and overseas projects. Through activity, they discover a great deal about themselves, and God, and what it means to be a Christian in the world today.

EVANGELISM: NETWORKER RECIPES

Outreach-focused networkers see themselves forming church around community, rather than the other way around. It is a 'fresh' approach to evangelism, found in various expressions of emerging church, journey church, and alternative worshipping communities. As such, it is not overtly evangelistic, with personal challenges offered rarely, if ever. Allowing the transient aspects of evangelism to dominate discipleship may leave little room for evangelism at all, in the end.

Nevertheless, good recipes for evangelism among networkers will make use of the many hubs in which they have membership, in order to build personal connections between them. Good recipes will involve the arts, creativity, friendship groups, and fresh approaches to friendship evangelism. Personal invitation, 'bringing a friend', and web networking will yield far better response than blanket invitations. Events will offer ample opportunity for individual, experiential encounters with God. On this count, it is important that these encounters are directed and have content. Otherwise, our recipes will foster little other than some nebulous New Age spirituality masquerading as Christianity.

Something that means anything, because you can read whatever you like into it, isn't worthy of life commitment. But the networker's willingness to be vulnerable can help others to be more open to the possibility of God at work in their lives, and in the world. There is also great potential for evangelism through social witness, as networkers become involved in political issues and organizations. At the same time, they need to be reminded that social action is a partner to evangelism, and not its substitute.

The feast is for the hungry, the poor, the outcast, and the marginalized. It is also for the banker, the prostitute, the Prime Minister, and the Queen. We are all sent out to invite others to the feast. What's standing in our way?

5

Beyond the Naked Chef

Beyond the Naked Chef

Count the cost

Let's say you want to take your loved one or a good friend out to dinner for their birthday. You'll probably think about where you'll go that serves good food that they will like. You'll also consider the ambiance of the place, and whether it's appropriate to the occasion. This time you decide to try a new place you've heard friends and colleagues raving about, but you've never been there yourself. It's a bit risky, but hey, you're an adventurer! You'll think about what you should wear, and might even decide to splash out on a new shirt, or a great pair of shoes. You'll phone ahead to reserve a table, just to be sure. You get there and order a nice bottle of something, and then peruse the menus. 'Order anything you want, it's your birthday,' you say generously.

Everything's perfect. Soft music, happy chatter, great smells emanating from the kitchen. You've managed to get the prime table, at the window overlooking the river. You toast your guest, and then turn to peruse the menu, congratulating yourself on the divine execution of a perfect plan. But suddenly, your parmesan breadstick – the best breadstick you've ever tasted in the world, ever

⌐ is stuck in your throat, and your heart almost jumps out of your chest. 'Are you OK?' your friend asks, as you choke. You manage to grunt a reply while sipping some water for support. It's not the glorious seafood, the lobster thermidor, or the noisettes of spring lamb that cause your reaction. No, in all of your planning, you never thought to ask anyone *how much it costs* to dine in this wonderful restaurant! Now it's too late, and you need to plan how to (a) feign illness and go home, (b) arrange with the manager to wash dishes every evening for the next week, or (c) sneak a fly into your food and claim it was there all along. Or, you could just run out screaming and flee the country. The little room you have left on your credit card combined with your entire bank overdraft aren't enough to get you out of this one. You should have counted the cost *before* you went ahead with your plan.

Jesus talks about this very thing in Luke 14. He offers some tough teaching about not putting family or friends, or even our own lives, ahead of following him. 'Whoever does not carry the cross and follow me cannot be my disciple. For which of you, intending to build a tower, does not first sit down and estimate the cost, to see whether he has enough to complete it? Otherwise, when he has laid a foundation and is not able to finish, all who see it will begin to ridicule him, saying, "This fellow began to build and was not able to finish."' Jesus reminds us that until we're ready to give up everything that we count as our own, we cannot be called his disciples.

JESUS REMINDS US THAT UNTIL WE'RE READY TO GIVE UP EVERYTHING THAT WE COUNT AS OUR OWN, WE CANNOT BE CALLED HIS DISCIPLES.

There is an immense cost of discipleship in a consumer culture. It makes the possibility of our salvation marvellous indeed! When the whole of our lives revolve around accumulating possessions, enjoying possessions, loving possessions, it is a crucial reminder that the future of the church depends on us counting the cost of discipleship and getting our priorities right.

What this means for us, as individuals, will vary. For many, it will mean surrendering our attachments to old ways of doing things. We will have to give up our possessiveness over programmes that have outlived their usefulness. It may mean releasing our sense of ownership over church furniture and buildings. It may feel insecure, and scary. But count the cost. To keep these things for ourselves and our own agendas, and not release them to Christ's control, is to underestimate the cost of discipleship today. Are we proud of our plush auditoriums, and our state-of-the-art multimedia equipment? We rightly wish to connect with a visual, entertainment culture. But have we counted the cost when we think of brothers and sisters in Christ who will not eat today while we install a new plasma screen in the lobby? We should not rest easy in our choices.

Our plans for evangelism in a brave new world will require negotiation and trade-offs. And as we mix and remix the store ingredients and fresh produce of church and culture together, we should not forget the radical call of Jesus to surrender everything. And let's face it – it belongs to him anyway. We're only on borrowed time. If we're not willing to give up everything we count as our own, we are not disciples in a position to make other disciples.

The dirty 'c' word is one that comes to mind here – commitment. It is a major theme of Jesus' teaching, and one that runs counter to a contemporary mindset. Jesus is seeking followers who will give up everything and follow him to the death. Now *that's* commitment. Believers in many parts of the contemporary world are asked to give up their lives for him every day. And we find it hard to give him five minutes.

The advent of the one-minute Bible for people who are time-poor, new church models where people don't have to meet together at all, Christians worshipping in pubs rather than in homes or meeting houses, large numbers of people who consider themselves 'Christian' but who show up for worship only once or twice a year – these are all examples of a church whose teeth have grown soft from suckling at culture's malnourishing teat. They are all examples of a lack of commitment on behalf of Christ's hangers-on, and without commitment, we are not taking up our cross, and we are not following him.

There was an ad for the Xbox gaming system when it first came onto the market which was brilliant, but sadly was banned (apparently somebody complained that it was distressing). The ad began with a woman screaming in labour pains as her baby is shot from her and through the open window of the hospital room. As the baby flies through the air at an increasing rate of speed, he changes. From an infant to a teenager, to a young adult, to an old man, who seizes up with a heart attack before slamming into a headstone and into the ground of a cemetery. 'Life is short. Play more,' were the words left on the screen.

We do need to learn to resist being slaves to the routines of life, and to make sure we have some time to 'play'. But play doesn't mean frittering away hours in front of a screen or slaving away to save for the next adventure holiday. We enjoy life most fully when we have a sense of purpose and direction, which orders our desires, and develops our priorities. In the church, we are most content when we know what our gifts are, and are given an appropriate opportunity to exercise them in the service of Christ. Commitment doesn't require a small group of people doing everything all the time while others barely turn up.

Pleas for better 'work-life' balance are nothing short of a call to reorganize priorities and commitments. For the Christian, work is not a negative thing that is endured to help us get on with 'real' life. Rather, work is part of life, where we can play, and be creative, even as we are committed to what we are doing. The biblical image is that of a bond-servant – not a Welcome mat that invites people to walk over and wipe their feet, but a willingness to surrender claims to self-indulgence for the good of others. Could it be that this is our contemporary cross, which Jesus invites us to take up as we follow him?

We need more solid commitment, by a wide range of people, if we are going to make a difference in this world for Christ, through our discipleship and evangelism. We need to rescue the word 'duty' from the rubbish bin of dirty words, so that we can strike a new balance between self-service and self-sacrifice. We need to see ourselves as the responsible, capable people that we are, with a lot to offer to ourselves, to Christ, to others.

This kind of commitment doesn't merely put Christ first, ahead of self, family, church, work, as though these things are unimportant to him. More accurately, it puts him first *in* everything. Because self, family, church, work, are important to him, he desires to be first *in* those things, not apart from them. Commitment means ordering our priorities in all spheres of life so that Christ is first *in* our work, *in* our families, *in* our churches, and *in* our own lives.

For some this might mean doing less in a particular sphere of life, while for others it will mean doing more. Commitment might mean doing less in the church but more at work to share your faith with colleagues. It might mean spending more intentional time with your family so that they learn what it means to be loved by Jesus. It might mean doing less at church and at work so that you can be a real presence in your neighbourhood. Or it might mean giving up your right to a holiday and going on an urban mission instead. Count the cost. Not to do it is to deny our purpose and call. It is to betray Christ, and his sacrifice which demanded a commitment beyond our imagining.

This is not a call to cease meeting together in church, as I have heard some do. Rather, it is a call to a life of integrity that worships well in community because it has experienced the depth of human need, and the power and love of Christ in various situations. The assembled meeting of believers is crucial to discipleship and evangelism in the contemporary world. We may well need to 'downsize' our programmes and meetings to release people for growth and mission. But we need to keep meeting together for our own edification, and that of others. The church is in a unique position to be able to model an alternative way of living to that of the mainstream of society, without sealing itself off completely. Demonstrating a community that can function without slavery to time, success, or money will offer a counter-cultural vision that connects with the situation of people today.

A RECENT SURVEY REVEALED THAT THREE-QUARTERS OF 16-YEAR-OLDS IMAGINE THAT THEY WILL PREFER TO WORK LONG HOURS IN RETURN FOR MORE PAY, RATHER THAN WORK FEWER HOURS FOR LESS PAY.

This is easier said than done. In fact, there is evidence that we'll have to swim very hard against the cultural tide. A recent survey revealed that three-quarters of 16-year-olds imagine that they will prefer to work long hours in return for more pay, rather than work fewer hours for less pay. As we become slaves to cultural success, we are less likely to have an alternative way of life to offer our society. There are a few, but not a lot, of creative solutions out there for how authentic, time-rich community might actually be embodied in the life of the church. But here's our chance to shine as lights. Here's a way we can really be salt in the world without dissolving in the tide of our culture. Let's take up this challenge, and be a movement for change in the values and priorities of our society. Maybe we'll need to start with small groups of like-minded people in covenant with one another. We'll need to think outside the box and inside the kingdom. It will cost. But the potential reward, both for our lives as disciples, and for our mission to the world, will be great. Is anyone willing to risk it?

Take the risk

Someone once asked me if I knew the difference between the church and *Jurassic Park*. I went for the bait and said, no, I didn't know. 'Well', I was told, 'one is a prehistoric fantasy land ruled by dinosaurs. And the other is a blockbuster Hollywood film directed by Steven Spielberg.' Ba-boom. And ouch.

We laugh at this joke, and feel its sting, because we're aware of how the world sees our churches. Many of the views they have are inaccurate, and we long to show them how the church actually has changed and developed. But the criticism hits close to home on some occasions, and we become forced to admit that even though God will build his church, it sometimes feels as though the gates of hell are prevailing against it in the western world.

This means that there is a lot at stake in reading our culture and getting the mission right. When we feel this pressure, we may become fearful, and cynical. We become the critics of the church *par excellence* in order to disarm the critics from without. We don't want to be grouped with those who are the target of derision in society, because we can see the problems too. We grow resentful of tradition, and sceptical of the efforts of others. We forget that we are the very thing that we criticize, and that it's up to us to do something about it. It's always easier to moan and complain about what's wrong than to participate positively in a solution.

Getting the mission right means putting aside our fear of being ridiculed, and being willing to take the creative risk. It means we have to risk failure, and maybe try over and over again, learning from our mistakes as we go. The important thing is not to give up, and to keep getting better. Real inventors of recipes do this very thing. They will take a simple dish and vary the ingredients, even slightly, and make the dish over and over again. They will try all the recipes they know for pastry. They will try them with lard, and with butter. They will use rice flour and corn flour, and wheat flour. They try it all again with more water and with less water. Finally, after a long season of experimentation, they will emerge with what they believe is the best recipe for the tastiest flakiest piecrust ever. And even then, they will always be on the lookout for a better one.

I've been told by many people in Britain that they didn't learn to cook with confidence because they were brought up during the war, when rationing meant that ingredients could not be wasted. Parents were unwilling to have their children experiment with making biscuits, because if it didn't work out, they wouldn't have any more sugar for a while. I'm grateful that as a child, even though ingredients in our house were sometimes a scarcity, I was encouraged to experiment, both with and without supervision. One day I decided I wanted to make fudge. I put the sugar in the pot, and even though the recipe told me to turn on the heat, I thought it would be better if I added some water before turning the burner up. Of course, the sugar boiled all day, and I never did get any fudge! But through experiments like that one, over time, I learned what ingredients blend together, and which ones clash. I learned when too much liquid would ruin a recipe and when there was enough. I still like to experiment, and I still get it wrong sometimes. But I have acquired a taste for adventure that keeps our supper table interesting, and developed the skills to prevent too much waste.

I fear that in our present climate of complaining about the church, we will lose our ability to experiment at a time when we need it most. We need to be able to try all sorts of different things, knowing that some won't work out, and others will. We need to be able to risk some resources here, and some energy there, in order to devise the best recipes possible for our culture today. We need to be able to take the risk that our whole lives might be spent in experimentation, and we still may not get it quite right. This is made all the more difficult because we are not accustomed to things taking time. We want instant success, and we want our recipes to be instantly recognized as wonderful. We want to be seen as the Jamie Olivers of the Christian world for bringing something fresh and new to the scene. It mitigates against risk and experiment for Christ's sake, and fosters experiment for our own sakes.

Our western culture has been described as a 'wannabe culture'. Our streets are filled with wannabes – wannabe rich, wannabe famous, wannabe Britney, wannabe Robbie. We have produced a generation of ambitious youngsters, but their ambition is sometimes misguided. They want to follow the latest trends, and to be seen with the right people. Many adults are the same. Don't go to her house, she's boring. Don't accept their invitation to dinner, they're not popular enough at work.

This unstable attitude can spill over into our Christian lives. It can wreak havoc on our discipleship, and our approaches to evangelism. We may soon find ourselves drowning in a wannabe culture inside the church. Wannabe a pop star worship leader, wannabe a famous personality, wannabe the coolest church around. Again, it's great to have ambition. But often our ambition is misplaced. We engage in a particular outreach because we think it will make us look good. Or we condescend to chat with some street people because it makes us feel noble. We turn down invitations to dine with the unpopular folks, and hang out instead with the ones on the ascendancy in the church. Worse than that, we put our leaders on pedestals that are so high, it becomes almost impossible for them not to lose their balance and fall.

If we hope to be successful in our discipleship and evangelism in this perishable culture, we have to mix it with the stabilizing ingredient called faithfulness. Faithfulness is willing to take risks, willing to be humiliated, willing to be last and least.

Again, in Luke 14, Jesus talks about a feast, a great feast. You'd think people would be chomping at the bit to get in, but the host, well, he can't have been the most popular guy in town. He sent out his invitations and laid the table. He laid the food out and had everybody's place card ready. But there was no one to be seen. So he sent his servant out to tell his guests that the meal was ready, but they all started to make their excuses. And what lame excuses they are! The first one tells him 'I've bought a piece of land, and I must go out and see it; please accept my regrets.' Another says, 'I've bought five yoke of oxen and I am going to try them out; please accept my regrets.' Another one explains he can't come because he just got married. I suppose he never thought of bringing his wife along!

In one place where we lived, we had no idea how the local culture functioned over the holiday season. You know what I mean, every place seems to have its own customs for dealing with Christmas and New Year. As we were new to the area, we thought it would be great to put on a huge spread of food, and invite the whole community to an open house on New Year's Eve. That way, if they had plans to go out, or to spend time with family, they could just drop in for a little while and be on their way. We bought heaps of food, and spent all day preparing cheesecakes and chocolate éclairs. When the time came for the guests to arrive, we lit some candles and waited. And waited. And waited. Eventually a few people came and went, but only a few. We were upset especially that the food would be wasted, and so we started to phone some local youth whom we knew would be watching videos together. They were happy to receive whatever food we could give them, and they feasted that night.

You've heard the excuses – 'I've got to wash my hair,' 'I've got to see my family,' 'I've got to go away for the weekend.' You worked hard to make the programme succeed, and you thought you had everything right. The seeker service was planned, the publicity was professional, the band well-rehearsed, the message presented with drama and style. But no one came. Well maybe one or two out of the ordinary, but that's all.

The man that Jesus told us about didn't let lack of attendance discourage him. He told his servant to 'Go out at once into the streets and lanes of the town and bring in the poor, the crippled, the blind, and the lame.' He did that, and there was still more room, so the master sent him out to compel anyone who would from the roads and streets to come and fill his house, and eat his food. 'For I tell you, none of those who were invited will taste my food.'

What an indictment against the wannabes who thought they were too busy and too occupied to come to this man's banquet. No longer were they his friends. They took his hospitality for granted, and rejected it. They couldn't take up the invitation later; it was revoked.

In God's kingdom, who are we? We are the poor, wretched, and lame. It's the only way we can come to Christ, when we're humbled and admitting our need. And Jesus sends us out like the master sends out his servant. Too often, we go to the invited guests, and hear their excuses. 'Maybe later in my life.' 'I just don't get all this Jesus stuff.' 'My work is too demanding.' 'My family is busy with activities.' We are tenacious, and keep asking, keep inviting. We go back to the master and ask him to rearrange the feast to make it more attractive, more appetizing. We then return to the invited guests and plead with them again to come. We hang out with them, and try to see if we might bring them a picnic lunch from the master's table, but still there are only excuses. We shake our heads in despair at the food going to waste.

We forget that there may be others who will come and eat the food – others who we did not originally think to invite. They may be people who embarrass us, or are awkward, people we find difficult. They may be the people we consider unpopular, and wannabes who will never arrive. We need to be willing to share the feast with those who *do* want an invitation, rather than harp on at those who have already rejected it. We have to take the risk to step outside of our comfort zone, and associate with the wannabes of God's kingdom, rather than the wannabes of popular culture. It may make us unpopular, it may be tedious, it may seem that growth is too slow to measure. But that's the risk of humility that God calls us to take on.

Jesus told his disciples that if the world hated him, it would hate them. Why do we expect it to be any different?

We shouldn't be surprised to be the butt of jokes like Ned Flanders on *The Simpsons*. In some ways, it's right that ours is a faith that does not shy away from criticism. The risk we are asked to take in the western world is sometimes costly. I know of teachers who have lost their jobs for standing firm in their faith. At the same time, we must remember that the risks we take at the present time usually pale in significance next to the risks some of our brothers and sisters in the world have to take every day, just to live and work, and worship. We risk ridicule; many risk their lives.

When we do take this risk, of taking up the 'lowest place' at the banquet, Jesus assures us it is worthwhile. And he challenges us directly, 'When you give a luncheon or a dinner, do not invite your friends or your brothers, or your relatives or rich neighbours, in case they may invite you in return, and you would be repaid. But when you give a banquet, invite the poor, the crippled, the lame, and the blind. And you will be blessed, because they cannot repay you, for you will be repaid at the resurrection of the righteous.' It is a worthwhile risk. For it is the risk of righteousness. We may not appear to be on the top of the heap in this world, but God's kingdom turns the world upside-down.

The recipes that we must risk making are those that nourish and feed the needy, in body and in spirit. We cook for them recipes of liquid and solid, milk and meat, and we seek them out, and bring them back to the banquet. The needy are any who recognize their self-insufficiency, and desire God. They are those who aren't even wannabes, because they know they're never-gonnabe. Or they've come to see the meaninglessness of a wannabe culture but haven't been able to catch a glimpse of anything better ... till now.

Use the imagination

We are slowly getting to grips with the idea that as image-bearers of the Creator God, we too are creative. Being creative doesn't only refer to our ability to draw a picture of a person that doesn't resemble a stick-figure, or our relative merits as *Watercolour Challenge* contestants. It means we are able to imagine things that aren't visible, and put steps in place to make them concrete. It means we can see things differently from how they are, and we can engage the creative process of getting them there.

Despite his publicized faults, Walt Disney had a notoriously creative mind. He had ideas and thoughts and visions of all kinds of interesting, fascinating things. But he had no ability to make his dreams a reality. He could see where he wanted to go, but every time he tried to get there, he hit a wall. Strategic thinking wasn't his gift. He recognized this, and so partnered with his brother to form a successful business. His brother wasn't so good at envisaging the end-product, but he could imagine the way of getting to the place Walt described. So together they made Walt's ideas come to life, and they have touched billions of lives around the globe, through several generations.

We have a marvellous opportunity in the community of faith to develop these sorts of partnerships. Too often, the creatives hang together, and the business folks get on with business. In actual fact, where the two work hand-in-glove, great things are accomplished for the kingdom. Disciples know that they do not have all the gifts, and that they need one another to bring out the best in everybody. If we are going to devise recipes that connect with our culture today, we need to give our inventive minds some creative licence, and a commitment to partner with them in making their visions a reality.

God is in the business of making our dreams come true. I'm not talking here about our dreams of the perfect relationship, or the three-bedroom detached bungalow, or the Christian theme park with its 'Hallelujah waterslide'. What I'm talking about is the corporate dream of the people of God for salvation and wholeness. The word for wholeness in Hebrew is shalom. It is often translated as 'peace' but it is a peace that goes beyond an absence of violence or fear. It is a state of existence that embraces all of life, from our relationship with God, to our lives together in community. It represents completeness. God's people in the Old Testament had a dream of wholeness. They longed for a Messiah who would bring this wholeness to their lives, and restore their broken relationship with God. They were a people in exile, away from the land that they loved, and the God that they worshipped.

As people in exile do, they lamented. But they didn't simply complain. They caught a vision of how things could be different beyond the circumstances they were in. Beyond the horizon of what was apparent to them in their place of despair, they saw a Saviour. It wasn't an invention of their own minds, but a picture of God's plan that longed to unfold around them. Eventually, it did unfold. What they could not see, but believed in, came to pass. And things that were previously invisible to them, became visible for the first time for all to see. When Jesus was born in Bethlehem, their dreams began to come true.

Colossians tells us that Jesus is the image of the invisible God, the firstborn over all creation. Although God is spirit, and those who worship him must worship in spirit and in truth, he is also a God who can picture invisible things for us. As the Creator God of the universe, he made many wonderful things that reveal his goodness. But he went even further than that. In Jesus Christ, the Father God gave us an image, a snapshot, an embodiment, of his love for us. The dreams of the Israelites for shalom have been fulfilled in Christ. He is shalom for us. And he is still in the business of making dreams come true.

But what dreams? What do we long for from the perspective of the church today? We have seen the vacuity of the wannabe culture. And yet we find it hard to accept that the church we have is as good as it can be. We have to learn the hard lesson of discipleship that allows us to accept the church as it is, and yet hope for more.

I once found myself in ministry in a church that by all worldly standards was pathetic. The body was elderly and worn out. The building was immense, cold, and empty. The few who were there were not interested in plans for growth or outreach. After exhausting every plan and idea I could come up with, I despaired. Mostly I complained to God. 'Why have you sent me to such a God-forsaken place, Lord?' I thought my gifts were being wasted, that I should be leading a big church into successful new ventures in mission. My imagination was being cast into exile. My ideas had come to nothing. In the midst of my wilderness wanderings, I began to read Dietrich Bonhoeffer's little book *Life Together*.

> HOW CAN YOU EXPECT GOD TO ENTRUST YOU WITH GREAT THINGS, HE WROTE, IF YOU DESPISE THE SMALL THINGS HE HAS ALREADY GIVEN TO YOU?

As I read the book, I became deeply challenged by a number of profound things that the Nazi camp prisoner wrote about Christian discipleship for individuals in community. In particular, one passage cut to the heart. How can you expect god to entrust you with great things, he wrote, if you despise the small things he has already given to you? Indeed, how could I? What right did I have to demand of God that he lead me into wonderful opportunities, if I hated the opportunity he had already set before me? Then and there, I knelt in prayer, and committed myself to that small group of people. God's people. Ever since that day I have been passionate about the small church. Good things can come in large packages, but they also come in tiny ones. Like mustard seeds.

Jesus reminded us that the kingdom of God starts small, like a mustard seed. It is the tiniest of all seeds, but when it grows, it becomes a shrub. It develops into a tree that is big enough for birds to build nests in its branches. The kingdom of heaven is like yeast, those tiny little grains of activity, that are mixed into a large amount of flour. And yet even a little is able to work through the entire batch. When you hold a mustard seed or a grain of yeast in your hand, it's exciting to imagine what it will become.

The important thing is that whether our immediate opportunities are big or small, we imagine the future that God has in mind for us. It is easy to dream our own dreams, but the ones that God guarantees are the ones that he dreams for us. We need to engage the resources of imagination to picture how we look from his perspective, and not simply from the perspective of the values of this world. The temptation is to make Christianity palatable to as many people as possible. We can quickly lose our distinctiveness, and allow the culture to overtake us, rather than work our influence through our culture. We're told by Jesus to be salt in the world. But if we are not focused, and spread ourselves too thinly, the taste of salt can become so watered down that it is almost indistinguishable.

At the end of Luke 14, Jesus laments the loss of distinctiveness that so easily envelops his people. 'Salt is good,' he says, 'but if salt has lost its taste, how can its saltiness be restored?' The answer is obvious. It can't be restored. The salt isn't good for anything any more. 'It is fit neither for the soil nor for the manure pile; they throw it away.' Our own vain imaginings can lead us down a path of despair. But connecting with God's plan for a real future guides our imagination to envision a future and a hope. We embody his future in the here and now and help the world to imagine how things can be different. As those who bear the image of God, we have to allow him to imagine his future for the world through us. By not growing discouraged, and cynical, and by living as a people of hope, we are resisting those aspects of our culture that rob us of our saltiness. By surrendering our desire for control, and allowing him to creatively imagine his future through our lives, we signal our availability to be yeast and mustard seeds. Sensitivity to Christ's special presence with his disciples in the world keeps us salty through and through.

But the question remains, how do we connect with the future that God imagines? How do we distinguish his real ideas from our hollow dreams? For one thing, we need to foster our awareness of Scripture and keep in mind the overall patterns of history and human existence that are described there. Beyond that, we can do our best to understand where our world is going, where culture is headed next. Because culture is a human creation, it is dynamic and in constant transition. This is especially so in the contemporary world where things change overnight. I read with amusement the letter in *The Times* from the man who lamented the demise of the VCR just as he had learned how to operate one.

Part of the prophetic gift in today's world entails an ability to read and understand the trends, and imagine the influence they will have on culture, in order that we might know how to respond as a church. We're generally not very good at this as Christians. Our biblical reflection lags far behind most cultural developments. It seems hardly able to anticipate them. The need is not so much for more individual seers to share what the Lord dropped on them out of the blue. Instead we're desperate for communities of informed prophets, who know the Scriptures, understand what is happening in the world, and who can prayerfully imagine the future and give us some alternative visions. It's not so much a gift of heavenly knowledge that we need, as one of applied wisdom.

So we should not shy away from gathering all the information we can in order to assess where our culture is headed. As Jesus told his disciples to look around them and read the signs of the end, so we can learn to look around us, and begin to read the signs of his presence, his plans, his judgements, and his grace. By reading the signs of the times, we can imagine various ways our future might unfold, and prepare for them in ways that are faithful to our calling to *be* disciples and to *make* disciples.

In John Naisbitt's book *Megatrends*, published at the advent of the 1980s, he predicted what he believed would be the major cultural shifts that would take place in the coming decade. Based on his knowledge of society, business, and culture, he suggested we would move from an industrial society to an information society, from a culture where technology is forced to one where people are high-tech and high-touch; we would move from nationally based economies to a world economy; our culture would become less short-term oriented and more long-term focused; organizations would become more decentralized; people would reject institutional help in favour of self-help; we would look for more direct action in our politics rather than leave someone else to do everything on our behalf; we would abandon hierarchical structures for networks; there would be a global shift from the north to the south; and we would shift from making either / or choices to demanding both / and in our choices.

With a couple of notable exceptions, it is difficult to fault Naisbitt's predictive abilities. Those business leaders who paid attention to the anticipated social trends would have found themselves well-positioned to profit from the cultural shifts that took place. Many churches paid scant attention to this helpful imagination.

The trends anticipated in the revival of *Megatrends* at the beginning of the 1990s were slightly less accurate, but there is broad agreement that many of them were significant to at least some degree during the decade. That the nineties would be the age of biology, and that we would experience the triumph of the individual in society were dead right. But so what? All of that won't help us now.

Nevertheless, there are organizations still in the business of tracking trends and predicting futures. The world of commerce depends on them. Organizations like Sociovision in the UK conduct studies and research, and produce information from its think-tank for those who will pay top price for its visions of tomorrow. Similarly, there are networks of people, including Christians, who make it their business to understand where things in our culture are headed, in order that we might be prepared for them as the church. For example, *The Tomorrow Network* brings people together across business, government, and faith groups to consider trends and alternative visions of the future. We can draw on resources like these in order to see where our culture is headed. We can borrow this knowledge, and use it with wisdom.

As a brief exercise, let's look at one of the predicted trends and its possible outcomes. Let's consider what it might mean for the church.

Culture watchers know that our consumer culture is the predominant influence in society as a whole. At the moment, shopping malls have generally outdone the high street, but shoppers are demanding a more and more specialized and individualized service. This may have at least two possible outcomes. Either more people will demand personalized service through online shopping, leaving the malls as empty ghost towns, or the high street will be revitalized as specialist shops move in to position themselves in an emerging niche market. Or, we may simply have larger malls that will cater for all tastes, with niche shops and department stores increasingly gathered under one roof.

As the church, this leaves us with a dilemma. On the one hand, people will be more and more demanding of products and services to be tailored to their specific needs. This could result in 24-hour one-stop church shops that offer wholistic massage therapy in one room, and a collective worship high in another. There could be services throughout the day, chosen to co-ordinate with your mood and the company you keep. Or, churches could specialize, seeking to cater for a particular niche group such as women with careers in tree-felling, or teenage skater boys from the east side of town.

An alternative vision for the church in this scenario is that our buildings would all close and be sold off, as people connect to Christian communities online. We would bring the church to their living rooms and studies, as they log on for worship and fellowship. Neither of these alternatives seems cheering from a biblical point of view. It seems that the church isn't called to cater for every little felt need of every individual. Indeed, it would be impossible to do such a thing. In this case, is it better to change in order to conform to the culture, or to persevere in what we recognize may be a counter-cultural stance? If we opt for the latter, we may well find ourselves in consistent decline, and increasingly distant from our culture. It seems we'd better give in. Ignore the warning of Dean Inge, who told us that the church who married the spirit of the age would find herself a widow in the next.

But wait – use your imagination! It may well be that in such a consumerist future, people will be desperate for human contact, living as they do in a virtual world. A significant increase in one-person households will mean there may also be lots of isolated individuals, who will need a place of welcome and warmth, unable to find authentic community anywhere else. It could be that the church that remains faithful to a biblical vision will find its place of relevance as a meeting-place for disparate and diverse people, who need someone to laugh with them and cry with them, to share their joy and sorrow, more than they need yet another Reiki treatment. If we can imagine this future, we can begin to prepare ourselves as individuals to network with those who might have such a desire. We can also plan our church programme to key into this reality, by equipping and releasing individuals and groups, and by directing the resources of the community to nurture and grow the community, in quality and not only in quantity. Using the resources of knowledge and insight, together with biblical conviction, enables us to inform and direct the imagination to write recipes that work for discipleship and evangelism in the real world.

This is only one small example of possible future trends, and how the church might respond. We have to be able to constantly read what is happening in the world, to describe new ways of doing things, and then be able to picture in the mind's eye what the results and consequences will be. Thankfully, it doesn't take a genius to read the trends of culture. Anyone who is motivated to do it can do it. You need to read the newspaper, watch at least a little TV, and catch some of the latest films and albums. You need to do these things with a critical, biblically informed mind, always asking yourself, 'So what?' 'They've learned to map the human gene – So what?' '*The Lord of the Rings* was one of the greatest blockbuster movies of all time – So what?' It's not enough just to take it in or participate in it. You've got to think about it. You've got to ask the questions.

Here's a list of things to look out for. When you encounter ideas or read the newspaper, ask lots of questions. What does the Bible have to say about this? What are the implications for our society in the short-term? In the long-term? How would a disciple of Jesus respond? How will this affect the way I try to share Jesus with others? And praying for some God-wisdom along the way will not be misplaced.

- What are the latest scientific discoveries?
- What's happening in the universities?
- What are the 'philosophers' saying?
- What is happening historically?
- What are the artists doing?
- What does the global picture look like?
- Who has power?
- Who wants power?
- What are the sociologists telling us about ourselves?
- What does the Bible say about human nature?

It may seem daunting, even overwhelming, at the moment. But you'll find that as you engage this exercise on a regular basis, you'll soon begin to do it automatically. It will become second nature to you. Even if you simply have some of the questions habitually in mind when you look at the adverts on the billboards as you drive to work, or listen to the radio, or go shopping, you'll soon find yourself able to read and predict trends in a way that will amaze your friends with your prophet-like ability to see the future. You could even keep a notebook, and get together on a regular basis with others in your church to discuss the trends in culture, and what you think it means for your church's discipleship and outreach programme. Churches could do worse than to have a 'think-tank' forum, whose job it is to engage some creative strategic thinking about the future, and what it means for the church now. They could focus both on broad trends and on cultural shifts, and on local developments and community transitions. It might not only be productive in terms of discipleship and evangelism, but it could be a lot of fun!

Enjoy the conversation

Two dinner parties, two different situations. At the first table, you're a guest of a work colleague whom you don't really know very well. As it turns out, you don't know any of the other guests very well either. You feel awkward, and uncomfortable. You make a few false starts at conversation, but it's tough. Getting anything more than a grunt out of the guy slurping his soup is a Herculean task. The woman on the other side is talkative, but in fact, she won't shut up. She's been going on and on, giving you every sordid detail of her cat's killing escapades. If you had the feline within reach, you fear you might have one yourself. She seems not to care or even notice that you glazed over ages ago, and have contented yourself with making designs in the breadcrumbs that fell between your bowl and the edge of the table. The evening won't end soon enough for you.

At the second table, you're with your best and oldest friends, all gathered in one place. There's much noise and laughter, as you tease and insult each other, and share stories from work and home. You are so comfortable here that you don't think about conversation as an effort. It flows freely, naturally. You know you're accepted here, even when you say outrageous things, or when somebody else insists you'll be fired for the practical joke you played on your boss at work. You're very contented here, and so enjoy the communication, the food, the company, that you wish it never had to end.

In the first situation, you wonder why you accepted the invitation in the first place. You have little in common with the people there, and yet, you want to connect with them, on some level. You know you'll probably never be best friends, but still, it's an opportunity, isn't it? You try and make the best of it, because you never know when there might be an open door to say something good about Jesus. You never know when people are quietly watching you because they know you're a Christian. In the second – you're comfortable and accepted but less likely to say anything about your faith because some of them are not Christians. They're your good friends, so they know that Jesus is important to you, but you respect them and don't want to push your beliefs on them.

THIS IS THE PARADOX OF MUCH OF OUR EVANGELISM TODAY. WE ARE SURROUNDED BY PEOPLE WE LOVE, AND WHO LOVE US, BUT WHO DO NOT KNOW CHRIST.

This is the paradox of much of our evangelism today. We are surrounded by people we love, and who love us, but who do not know Christ. These are the people who accept us no matter what. The ones we're related to haven't any choice! And yet, we'll struggle and strain to witness for Christ with those we hardly know, while ignoring the fact that we're surrounded by opportunity in the faces and hearts of those we know best.

We can learn to let Christ flow naturally into the conversation; he's not an agenda we're pushing, just the way we see the world. If you're skipping church to do something for your brother-in-law, don't leave him with the impression that your religious life is expendable whenever something better comes along. Either tell him you'll help him after church because that's important to you, which will witness to your level of commitment to Christ, or if you do decide to spend the time with him instead, make sure he knows why. 'You know I normally would be at church this morning, but I decided it was important to be here for you as part of my commitment to Christ.' So what if he thinks you're a freak? At least he'll know the Jesus freak will be there for him.

To skip an important community vision day at church to play a round of golf with non-Christian friends is justifiable only if you actually introduce Jesus into the conversation. Otherwise, they see you only as a guy like them who would rather play golf and have a round at the clubhouse than hang out with a bunch of religious weirdos. It doesn't necessarily bring them closer to the kingdom.

If we are going to have a real conversation with our culture about Jesus, we have to surrender the desire to be 'normal'. I recently heard a group of young Christians bemoan the fact that they just want to be normal, live normal lives, go out on a Saturday night like normal people, dance on the table, like normal people do. I felt their longing for acceptance, but I believe they will have to give up the illusion of normalcy. To be a Christian in today's world is not normal. The things that define a Christian, and Christian belief, themselves are enough to set us apart as abnormal. If our dearest desire is to be 'normal' we will have to give up being Christians.

This is what integrity as disciples requires, and it spills over to our evangelism. What's attractive about a faith you're embarrassed to own? What's enticing about something that doesn't make you any different from those around you? If you're just like them, why should they want to be just like you? For one thing how do they know you're a Christian, and why should they want to be a Christian if it doesn't make their lives any different? If we are normal, we are to be pitied. Our Christian discipleship is nothing but a waste of time, energy, and money. Or, if our discipleship is simply about doing good work, why not join Oxfam instead? You have your charity work and I have mine. If your Jesus is not worth introducing to all your friends, then he's not the real thing.

The apostle Paul was willing time and again to encourage believers to follow his example, as he followed Christ's. He further exhorted the members of the church to be examples to one another, and to those in their culture. In other words, to put it very basically, we are to let our light shine in this world. Since the world is often dark, the light is going to stand out. It will draw attention. Some will complain about it, because it will illumine the nature of their ill-behaviour. Some will try to extinguish it. A few will ignore it. If we are human beings, living in this world, then we are as normal as we're going to be. Being a Christian makes us abnormal. And we should be willing to acknowledge that in our living and in our conversations.

For example, the call to renounce worldly success, and to seek after justice, to identify with the marginalized of our society, is not normal. To be a humble community of service is not normal. To welcome strangers, give sacrificially, to serve Christ and not consumerism, is not normal. To embark on initiatives that address the core issues in our neighbourhoods and communities is not normal. The call to discipleship is radical enough to reshape our lives so that we find ourselves completely out of step with those around us. We need to see this as a good sign of Christ's life at work in us. And we need to acknowledge that we cannot be a mission-shaped church without being first a disciple-shaped church.

This is not to say that we will be so different that we cannot communicate with those who do not share our faith commitment. In fact, we are obligated to find ways of communicating afresh with our culture, which is really what this book is all about. John Stackhouse calls it 'speaking in tongues', how we learn to speak with love to the culture in which we live. But I think we need to think more in terms of listening and speaking, a two-way or multi-directional dialogue, rather than simply laying out our wares and seeing who buys them.

H. Richard Niebuhr referred to this as learning to 'look at' and 'see with' our culture. This is a helpful distinction, and I think we need to appreciate both aspects. Some theologians and Christian leaders today are challenging us to 'see with' our culture rather than 'look at' it. I will explain why I think we must hold the two together.

An artist paints a picture of Christ. The picture is of a naked form on a cross. It is shocking, not because the form is naked, but because it is a woman. Looking at the painting brings a strong reaction, and objection. 'Jesus wasn't a woman! The artist is making Christ in her own image! What kind of bleeding-heart liberalism is this!' But pause for a moment. Instead of looking at the painting, see with it, to the world. What is it saying about the experience of woman in society? What is it communicating about woman's desire to be identified with Christ? What is it portraying about marginalization and exclusion? When we look *with* the painting, the world looks different than it did before. We may even gain a new insight into the work of Christ by seeing the cross with the artist.

But I'm not confident that seeing *with* our culture is sufficient. It may give us new insights, it may help to develop and mature our faith. It challenges and stretches us, and the way we understand our culture. But there are no tools provided for critiquing what we see. How can we know which of the things we see when we look with culture are real and true? We can have empathy, but no sense of direction about how our faith matters in different contexts. In one episode of *The Simpsons*, Bart puts on a pair of glasses that help him 'see the world through the eyes of a drunk'. As he peers through the lenses, desperate people appear happy, a messy world looks bright and cheerful, and members of the opposite sex appear definitely more attractive. Bart is *seeing with* the drunk. But without *looking at* the world without the glasses, he has no sense of how things really are.

When we watch an episode of *Friends*, or see a film at the cinema, we find it easy to enter the world of the director, and see the world with him. We identify with the characters and some of the situations, or we are entertained by what we see. Sometimes, while seeing the world with them, we gain a new insight that challenges our ethics, or stirs our faith. But very often, we don't think about the experience enough to critique it – to discover what is valuable and what is not. We entrust our emotions and experience to the director, but without 'looking at' the film, we have no way of knowing whether our trust has been misplaced. Seeing with the director or the artist can give us insight, but not understanding; empathy, but not discernment.

So let us return to the painting of the crucified woman. We push ourselves past our initial objections to see the world with the artist. We see some things in a way we haven't before. But we don't walk away yet. Instead, we now step back and 'look at' the piece, in light of what we have seen with it. Why did the artist paint this piece? What was her experience of life that led her here? Is it an authentic representation of human experience? Is it accurate to our understanding of the cross in Scripture? *Looking at* the piece, after we have *seen with* it, deepens our encounter with culture, and opens up the conversation. It means that the dialogue is one of listening and talking, rather than simply one or the other.

A dialogue implies that both parties have something to learn from the other. It implies a certain openness to the concerns and life experience of the other. It acknowledges the God-given responsibility and dignity of the other, and it employs the networks of relationships that we already have in sharing our faith with the people we know best. A dialogue is a conversation that lets community emerge and develop according to the life experiences of its members, but with some structure and with some direction. It is comfortable with a degree of diversity, while offering some limits to diversity.

The people of God are a diverse people. Handling the diversity of the people of God in community can be a challenge. For many, diversity produces insecurity and fear that cause them to react in anger or denial. They may display a lack of patience with new ideas, especially if they have had some measure of power in the community of faith. Others may find it difficult to accept diversity as a reality of contemporary life, and find it difficult to do things in a way that draws others in rather than excludes them. A music group has led the worship for many years, in a typical evangelical style. But transitions in the community have brought many new members from Africa and Asia. The music that suits their voices and experience is quite different from what the congregation is used to. The music group ignores the changes that have taken place, and refuses to accept the new reality. The leader is not comfortable with a change. The team dwindles. Embracing diversity could have brought new life to the group, but a denial of diversity has excluded the participation of new people in the worshipping life of the church. Our fear of diversity is challenged by the marvellous opportunity it represents to display the gift of unity that is a gift of the kingdom of God. Though we are different, we belong together.

In today's world, we need desperately to learn to dance with diversity. Dancing with diversity rejects a Jesus-plus gospel, that is, a gospel that demands people adhere to belief in Jesus plus some other thing. You belong only if you believe in Jesus plus speaking in tongues, Jesus plus lava lamps, Jesus plus prayer book. Dancing with diversity accepts the new and sees unity as a gift rather than an achievement. It confronts exclusion, and celebrates difference. It is joyfully re-creative.

Dancing with diversity means learning to see with and look at people who are different from ourselves. It means learning to engage in real dialogue with them as a manifestation of the unity we have in Christ. I was recently challenged by a brother in Christ who said that dialogue is a manifestation of disunity, and we should refrain from it. To the contrary, I argued. The fact that we dialogue as Christians means that we know we belong together. Our dialogue is itself a manifestation of our unity, and we need to learn to do it better, and become more comfortable with it. Pretending we have no differences is a dishonest expression of unity. Acknowledging that we have differences, together with a willingness to talk about them, is the beginning of learning to dance with diversity.

But where do we begin? What are some of the possibilities for dialogue between Christians? Well, quite obviously, we can learn to search the Scriptures together, and account for why we understand some of them differently. We can listen to others, and tell others. We can identify points of agreement and disagreement, and account for them. We can commit to further study and dialogue where we still differ, and learn to stop and celebrate successful dialogue.

Doing this as Christians will help us to grow in maturity of faith. It will help us know more about why we believe what we believe. It will develop our confidence in what we believe, even as we learn to be humble in conversation with those who believe differently on a particular point. It will remind us that God is bigger than all of our explanations of him, and yet, he desires to be known by us.

When we learn to dialogue together as Christians, we are challenged to engage in that process with those who aren't. We'll be much better at animating conversation at the dinner table where we're comfortable, and at the one where we're not. We'll be ready to serve up dishes that our guests appreciate, and some they won't. In both cases, it will be hearty, nutritious food that nourishes the soul, and grows the community of faith. And we'll enjoy the meal and the company of friends and strangers, because we won't simply be slaving in the kitchen any more. We'll be at the table, relaxed and conversing with ease. Because we know the recipes are good ones, and the Master Chef can be trusted.

In the end, it's pretty straightforward. Assemble your ingredients: examine the store cupboard, make sure the essential ingredients are up to date and well-stocked; then consider carefully the seasonal produce you will be working with today. Think about your guests, and suitable recipes. Stir gently. Experiment. Learn more about the ingredients. Experiment some more. Be creative, imaginative. Set the table. Lay out the food. Send invitations. Bring friends. Share the feast.

Bon appetit!